ULTIMATE
VEG

FLATIRON
BOOKS
NEW YORK

JOHN HAMILTON

1963–2019

Shortly after the last shoot day for this book, our long-standing art director and dear friend, John, unexpectedly passed away. He taught me publishing, stood by my side on every shoot, watched and tasted every dish of every book for 21 years, and was a gentle Glaswegian giant in the world of design. He generously gave so many opportunities to designers, photographers, artists and illustrators, and his passion for art and reimagining books of all kinds in extraordinary ways was unprecedented.

Me, my team and all my family at Penguin Random House salute you, John, for everything you have given us. Our hearts are broken, but you will always inspire us, and, as you would say . . . one love.

So much love to John's wife, Claire, and their wonderful kids, Sadie and Angus. xxx

CONTENTS

VEG POWER!

I'm fairly sure that if you've picked up this book and are reading these words, you're already asking yourself a few questions about the food you eat. All of us are aware that we need to eat more veg, and of the extraordinary health benefits attached to doing so. But, in a busy, fast-paced life where meat is so convenient and available on every corner, the question is – can veg dishes really cut the mustard? Can they be truly tasty and make you feel satisfied and happy? I believe that the answer is a gigantic YES! So, with that in mind . . . welcome to the wonderful world of delicious food that just happens to be meat-free.

This is a glorious veg-based cookbook, written by me – a meat lover who will absolutely not compromise on flavor. We humans are creatures of extreme habit, and the concept of change, even positive, challenges all of us. Most of us buy the same foods week in, week out – sound familiar? So, embracing this book for what it is, disarming yourself and opening your mind to trying new things by celebrating the huge bounty of veg, fruit, herbs, spices, pulses, nuts and seeds on offer, can only be a good thing. You can find so much exciting produce in standard supermarkets these days (let alone farmers' markets and beyond), and if you shop smart and surf the seasons, you should be quids in, so there's really no excuse . . . especially with this book in your hands! I hope it helps to break the mold.

EVERYONE'S WELCOME

On the pages that follow, I want to show you just how tasty and comforting veg-based meals can be when given the respect and thought they deserve. And I also want to stamp out any pre-existing prejudices around food choices. This book is not just for vegetarians: everyone's welcome – especially your classic meat eater who might be stuck in a bit of a rut but knows that they could, and should, be welcoming more veg into their diet. I designed these recipes to leave you feeling full, satisfied and happy – and not missing the meat from your plate. Whether you're looking to embrace a meat-free day or two each week, live a vegetarian lifestyle, or just want to try some brilliant new flavor combination, I believe this book will tick all the boxes and help you enjoy things you may never have tried before.

A quick note for all my strict vegetarian friends out there: you will see me mention Worcestershire sauce, pesto and Parmesan cheese (see page 268 for more info), among other things, in the ingredients lists on the recipe pages. Joyfully, we live in a time where you can source really good vegetarian versions or alternatives, so sit back, relax and fill your boots in a way that works for you.

I actually started writing this book eight years ago – it's been a real labor of love – but now is the time to publish it, accompanied by a beautiful new and exciting TV show. I've traveled halfway around the world to watch, listen and learn from some of the best veggie cooks on the planet, to really amplify flavor and scrumptiousness, and to give you beyond-tasty plates of food. Being able to finally publish this book is not only a real honor and a landmark moment for me, but also an indicator that the time is right and that veg-based cooking is becoming mainstream again. We might think that basing our meals around more veg and less meat is forward thinking, and is trendy or progressive, but I can assure you, if anything, it's looking back towards our grandparents and great-grandparents, who – by default – cooked this way. Without question, it was the norm, they knew what they were doing and we should absolutely take a leaf out of their book.

The recipes are a broad assortment of the food that I love to eat at home with my wife and kids, and are everything I would deliver flavor-wise in any other cookbook: they're dishes that make me feel energized, comforted, complete and full up. I'm not telling you to eat any of these meals because they're healthy (even though 70% of them are – see pages 286–93 for more nutrition info), I want you to eat them because you want to, and because they're delicious. As usual, they're all tried, tested and interrogated (and then tested again, just to be sure!), so they're the absolute best they can be. And for me, the beautiful thing about this book is that I can give you a really reliable, safe place to come for easy and delicious veg-based meals, put together with love, care and attention.

I've got lots of inspiration on the lunch and dinner front with easy pastas, soups and sandwiches, clever traybakes and one-pan wonders, as well as tasty curries, stews, pies, bakes, rice and noodle dishes, and burgers that'll knock your socks off. And that's not all – there's also an array of brunch and weekend nibbles to get your teeth into. I've tried to equip you with a myriad of modern meals, taking into account that you're probably incredibly busy, juggling 101 other things at the same time.

With that in mind, I've kept the visuals and words simple, clear, supportive and to the point, and have done my best to empower you with confidence, instead of baffling you with clutter and long, laborious lists or explanations. No barriers, just super-tasty, easy, accessible and affordable recipes, with veg as the main event. There's upfront nutrition info on every page so you can make fast, informed choices. Plus, I've given some extra tips on how I like to serve the dishes myself, as well as ways to tweak the recipes to include a whole array of beautiful veg.

NO BARRIERS, JUST SUPER-TASTY, EASY, ACCESSIBLE & AFFORDABLE RECIPES

Putting labels on food preferences, I have to say, frightens the life out of me – there are enough things in life that divide us, and I feel that food shouldn't be one of them. But it is. As far as I'm concerned, if it's good, it's good. Everyone's on their own food journey, and people are all at different stages. And that's OK! In the Oliver household we really try to eat veg-based meals at least three times a week, and the benefits to our health, as well as the planet, are clear to see. Promoting less meat (but better quality) and more veg is something I've always done: this is not a new thing for me – if you look at the index of any of my cookbooks, you're going to see a huge number of V symbols. Even so, I've been constantly asked by the public (sometimes berated!) to do a 100% veg-based cookbook, so here it is, guys – I hope you love it as much as I enjoyed making it.

CURRIES
& STEWS

CRISPY CAULIFLOWER KATSU

LIGHT & DELICATE CURRY SAUCE, FLUFFY RICE, LIME-PICKLED CHILIES

SERVES 6 | 1 HOUR 15 MINUTES

2 heads of cauliflower
   (1¾ lbs)

3 fresh mixed-color chilies

3 limes

1 cup all-purpose flour

3 large eggs

1¾ cups fine breadcrumbs

1 onion

4 cloves of garlic

2-inch piece of fresh ginger

1 carrot

1 bunch of fresh cilantro (1 oz)

olive oil

1 heaping teaspoon garam masala

1 teaspoon ground turmeric

3 teaspoons mango chutney

2¼ cups basmati rice

Preheat the oven to 350°F. Cut 6 chunky cauliflower slices, straight through the stalks, around 1 inch thick (use up the leftover stalkless cauliflower by making my Simple pickle, see page 252). Season the cauliflower slices all over with sea salt and leave aside (this will draw out the natural moisture). Meanwhile, finely slice the chilies and place them in a bowl with a pinch of salt. Finely grate over the zest of 2 limes, then squeeze over the juice and leave to lightly pickle.

Put ⅔ cup of the flour into one bowl, beat the eggs in another, and tip the breadcrumbs into a third. Coat the cauliflower slices in the flour, dunk in the beaten egg, then dip, press and coat in the breadcrumbs. Place on an oiled baking sheet and push down to compact. Bake for 45 minutes, or until golden and crisp.

Meanwhile, peel the onion, garlic, ginger and carrot, then finely chop with the cilantro stalks, reserving the leaves. Fry in a large pan on a medium heat with 1 tablespoon of oil and the spices for 15 minutes, stirring regularly. Stir in ⅓ cup of flour and the mango chutney, followed by 4 cups of boiling water. Whisk together, then simmer for 15 minutes, or to your preferred consistency, stirring occasionally. Taste and season to perfection with salt and black pepper. Cook the rice according to the package instructions, then drain. Serve the rice and sauce with the crispy cauliflower, chili pickle, lime wedges and reserved cilantro leaves.

> For that 1980s retro feel, mold the rice in small bowls like I've done here – it's pointless, but fun!

ENERGY	FAT	SAT FAT	PROTEIN	CARBS	SUGARS	SALT	FIBER
637kcal	9.2g	2g	23.6g	120g	16g	1.5g	10.4g

AMAZING VEGGIE CHILI

COMFORTING BLACK RICE, ZINGY CRUNCHY SALSA, CHILI-RIPPLED YOGURT

SERVES 4 | 1 HOUR 30 MINUTES

2 red onions

2 sweet potatoes (8 oz each)

3 mixed-color peppers

4 large ripe tomatoes

olive oil

1 teaspoon cumin seeds

1 teaspoon smoked paprika

4 cloves of garlic

1 lemon

1 x 15-oz can of cannellini beans

hot chili sauce

1⅓ cups black rice

1 bunch of fresh mint (1 oz)

4 small flour tortillas

¼ cup plain yogurt

Preheat a grill pan to high. Peel the onions, scrub the sweet potatoes and seed the peppers. Cut off a small chunk of each and put aside with 1 tomato (this is for the salsa later). Roughly chop the rest of the veg into 1½-inch chunks and halve the remaining tomatoes, then chargrill, working in batches.

Drizzle 1 tablespoon of oil into a large casserole pan over a medium-low heat and stir in the cumin seeds and paprika. Peel, roughly chop and add the garlic, finely grate in the lemon zest, and add the grilled veg bit by bit as they're ready, stirring regularly. Tip in the beans (juices and all), and 1½ cans' worth of water, then add around 1 tablespoon of chili sauce (or to your liking). Season with sea salt and black pepper and simmer for 30 minutes, or until thickened and reduced. Meanwhile, cook the rice in a pan of boiling salted water according to the package instructions. Pick 2 sprigs of mint leaves and very finely chop with the salsa veg, then toss with the lemon juice and season to taste with salt and pepper.

Warm the tortillas on the grill and ripple a good few shakes of chili sauce through the yogurt. Serve the chili with the black rice, salsa, yogurt and tortillas, and pick over the mint leaves. Enjoy!

> Using veg raw to make a salsa as well as cooking it in the stew is incredibly resourceful and delicious.

ENERGY	FAT	SAT FAT	PROTEIN	CARBS	SUGARS	SALT	FIBER
636kcal	9.1g	2.6g	18.3g	121.2g	26.4g	1.4g	15.3g

MY CAULIFLOWER TIKKA MASALA

PANEER, SPICED YOGURT MARINADE, CREAMY CASHEW & SAFFRON SAUCE

SERVES 4 | 45 MINUTES

2 oz unsalted cashews

1 pinch of saffron

1 tablespoon mango chutney

1 lemon

2 tablespoons plain yogurt

1 teaspoon smoked paprika

olive oil

7 oz paneer cheese

½ a head of cauliflower (14 oz)

1 knob of unsalted butter

1 cinnamon stick

3 cloves

3 cardamom pods

4 cloves of garlic

1 onion

2-inch piece of fresh ginger

2 tablespoons sun-dried
   tomato paste

4 sprigs of fresh cilantro

Put the cashews, saffron and mango chutney into a pitcher, cover with 3 cups of boiling water and leave to one side to soak. Preheat the broiler to high. Finely grate the lemon zest into a large bowl, add the yogurt, paprika, a pinch of sea salt and black pepper and 1 tablespoon of oil, and mix well. Chop the paneer into ¾-inch cubes and break the cauliflower into florets (roughly the same size), then toss in the marinade. Tip into a large roasting pan and broil on the middle rack for 12 minutes, or until beautifully golden and gnarly at the edges.

Put the butter and 1 teaspoon of oil into a large casserole pan on a low heat with the cinnamon and cloves, and bash the cardamom pods, adding just the inner seeds. Peel, finely slice and add the garlic, and cook for a few minutes, stirring occasionally. Peel the onion and ginger, roughly chop, then place in a blender with the tomato paste and a good splash of boiling water, and whiz to a paste. Pour into the pan and cook for 10 minutes, stirring regularly.

Tip the cashew mixture into the blender and whiz until super-smooth – you may need to work in batches. Pour into the pan, bring to a boil, then leave to tick away for 5 minutes, stirring occasionally. Stir in the paneer and cauliflower, season to perfection with salt and pepper, then place under the broiler. Once golden and bubbling, stir back through and pick over the cilantro leaves.

Delicious served with fluffy rice and wedges of lemon for squeezing over.

Swap the paneer for chickpeas and the cauliflower for squash for a different but equally delicious result.

ENERGY	FAT	SAT FAT	PROTEIN	CARBS	SUGARS	SALT	FIBER
426kcal	31.1g	13g	20.6g	17.5g	12.2g	0.8g	4.7g

STUFFED CURRIED EGGPLANTS

SPICED TAMARIND & PEANUT SAUCE, FRESH CILANTRO

SERVES 6 | 1 HOUR 15 MINUTES

1 onion

4 cloves of garlic

1½-inch piece of fresh ginger

½ a bunch of fresh cilantro (½ oz)

2 fresh red chilies

1 teaspoon each cumin seeds, mustard seeds, ground turmeric, garam masala, fenugreek seeds

1 big handful of fresh curry leaves

peanut oil

2 heaping tablespoons crunchy peanut butter

1 tablespoon mango chutney

2 tablespoons tamarind paste

12 finger eggplants (1¾ lbs total)

1 x 14-oz can of light coconut milk

8 oz ripe mixed-color cherry tomatoes

Preheat the oven to 375°F. Peel the onion, garlic and ginger, place in a food processor with the cilantro stalks and chilies (seed, if you like) and whiz to a fine paste. Put the spices and curry leaves into a 14- x 10-inch roasting pan on a low heat with 2 tablespoons of oil and fry for 1 minute, or until smelling fantastic, stirring constantly. Tip in the paste and cook for 5 minutes, or until softened, stirring regularly. Stir in the peanut butter, mango chutney and tamarind paste, season with a good pinch of sea salt and black pepper, then scrape into a bowl, adding a splash of water to loosen to a paste, if needed.

Leaving them intact at the stalk, cut the eggplants into quarters lengthways, rub and stuff them generously with all the paste, then arrange them in the pan (if using regular eggplants, simply trim then cut into ½-inch-thick rounds and sandwich the paste between them). Place the pan on a medium heat and fry for 5 minutes, turning halfway. Add the coconut milk, roughly chop and sprinkle over the tomatoes, season well with salt and pepper, and bring to a boil. Cover with aluminum foil and roast for 40 minutes, or until thickened and reduced, removing the foil halfway. Season to perfection and scatter over the cilantro leaves.

Always good with fluffy rice, pappadams, yogurt and extra fresh chili.

> Delicious and convenient made in advance and reheated when you need it – loosen with a splash of water, if needed.

ENERGY	FAT	SAT FAT	PROTEIN	CARBS	SUGARS	SALT	FIBER
221kcal	15.2g	5.6g	6.7g	15.9g	12.9g	0.9g	2.3g

SUPER-COMFORTING GUMBO

LOADS OF VEG, SMOKY SPICED GRAVY, PICKLED JALAPEÑO CHILIES

SERVES 6 | I HOUR 10 MINUTES

1 onion

3 cloves of garlic

3 stalks of celery

3 mixed-color peppers

peanut oil

3 heaping tablespoons
all-purpose flour

3 fresh bay leaves

3 sprigs of fresh thyme

½ teaspoon cayenne pepper

1 teaspoon smoked paprika

6 tablespoons red wine

1 x 14-oz can of quality plum
tomatoes

1 x 15-oz can of chickpeas

7 oz frozen peas

2 fresh jalapeño chilies

¼ cup red wine vinegar

7 oz okra

Peel and finely chop the onion, garlic and celery, and seed and roughly chop the peppers. Pour 3 tablespoons of oil into a large pan over a medium heat and mix in the flour to make a paste (loose roux). Cook until dark brown, stirring constantly so that it doesn't catch and burn. Add the chopped veg to the paste along with the bay leaves, then strip in the thyme leaves and cook for 20 minutes, or until softened and dark nutty brown, stirring regularly (give it some love).

Stir through the cayenne pepper and paprika, followed by the wine, and allow to reduce by half before scrunching in the tomatoes. Tip in the chickpeas (juices and all) and enough water to cover, then simmer over a medium heat for 25 minutes, or until reduced to your preferred consistency, adding the peas for the last 5 minutes. Season to perfection with sea salt and black pepper. Meanwhile, finely slice the chilies, place in a bowl, and stir in the vinegar and a pinch of salt to make a quick pickle. Dry-fry the okra in a large non-stick frying pan on a medium heat until lightly charred, then halve and scatter over the gumbo.

I like to serve the gumbo and pickle with fluffy rice and a handful of fresh parsley.

> Own your gumbo by surfing the seasons with pumpkin, squash, mushrooms, corn, zucchini. Use your imagination – it's a brilliantly flexible recipe.

ENERGY	FAT	SAT FAT	PROTEIN	CARBS	SUGARS	SALT	FIBER
250kcal	8.7g	1.7g	9.3g	32.3g	11.3g	0.6g	7.4g

AMAZING TOMATO CURRY

FRAGRANT SPICES, SAFFRON & COCONUT SAUCE, TOASTED ALMONDS

SERVES 4 | 40 MINUTES

2½ lbs ripe mixed tomatoes

1 pinch of saffron

¾ oz flaked almonds

4 cloves of garlic

1½-inch piece of fresh ginger

2 fresh red chilies

olive oil

1 handful of fresh curry leaves

1 teaspoon mustard seeds

1 teaspoon fenugreek seeds

1 teaspoon cumin seeds

1 onion

1 x 14-oz can of light coconut milk

2 teaspoons mango chutney

With the tip of a knife, prick the tomatoes, removing the cores from any larger ones. Carefully plunge them into fast-boiling water for 45 seconds, then drain and peel away the skin. Cover the saffron with 6 tablespoons of boiling water and leave to infuse. Toast the almonds in a large non-stick frying pan over a medium heat until golden, then tip into a small bowl and place the pan back on the heat.

Peel and very finely chop the garlic, ginger and chilies. Drizzle 1 tablespoon of oil into the pan, then add the curry leaves, followed by all the spices. Peel and quarter the onion, click apart into petals, then add to the pan with the garlic, ginger and chili and fry for 3 minutes, stirring constantly. Add the tomatoes, coconut milk and saffron water, then cover and simmer for 20 minutes, removing the lid and adding the mango chutney halfway. Season to taste with sea salt and black pepper, then scatter over the almonds. Serve with fluffy rice.

This curry goes up a level when tomatoes are at their most delicious, so make it in the summer with beautifully ripe tomatoes for the very best results.

ENERGY	FAT	SAT FAT	PROTEIN	CARBS	SUGARS	SALT	FIBER
208kcal	12.9g	6.1g	5.1g	19.7g	15.9g	0.2g	4.8g

BURNS NIGHT STEW & DUMPLINGS

CHUNKY ROOT VEG, HAGGIS SEASONING, CABBAGE & APPLE SLAW

SERVES 6 | 2 HOURS

10 oz celery root

10 oz rutabaga

3 carrots

olive oil

4 fresh bay leaves

6 oz silverskin pickled onions (drained)

½ teaspoon ground allspice

½ teaspoon ground cloves

⅓ cup pearl barley

1⅓ cups smooth porter

2 teaspoons blackcurrant jam

6 cups vegetable stock

2 cups self-rising flour

¼ cup unsalted butter (cold)

¼ of a red cabbage (7 oz)

1 eating apple

1 tablespoon red wine vinegar

1 teaspoon grainy mustard

Preheat the oven to 350°F. Peel the celery root and rutabaga and scrub the carrots, then roughly chop and place in a large casserole pan on a medium heat with 1 tablespoon of oil, the bay leaves, a pinch of sea salt and a generous pinch of black pepper. Drain the pickled onions and add with the ground allspice and cloves, then cook for 15 minutes, or until nicely golden, stirring regularly. Throw in the pearl barley, pour over the porter and leave to bubble and cook away, then add the jam and stock, and simmer while you make the dumplings.

Tip the flour into a bowl. Chop and rub in the butter, then mix in about 6 tablespoons of water, or just enough to bring it together into a pliable dough. Roll into 12 balls, then plop into the stew, shaking to coat. Drizzle lightly with oil, then cover and bake for 1 hour, or until the stew has reduced and the dumplings are golden and puffed up, removing the lid for the last 15 minutes to build some color. Meanwhile, very finely shred the cabbage and apple with good knife skills or on a mandolin (use the guard!). Toss with the vinegar and mustard, then season to perfection with salt and pepper.

Taste and season the stew, if needed, then serve with the dumplings and slaw.

> The dumplings will double in size as they cook, so make sure you've got enough distance between the stew and the lid of your pan.

ENERGY	FAT	SAT FAT	PROTEIN	CARBS	SUGARS	SALT	FIBER
424kcal	13.2g	5.1g	10.2g	67.1g	15.6g	1.9g	8.1g

THAI-STYLE MUSHROOM & TOFU BROTH

HOT, SOUR, SALTY & SWEET LIQUOR, FLUFFY CRISPY RICE CAKE

SERVES 6 | 25 MINUTES

olive oil

2¼ cups basmati rice

3¼ cups vegetable stock

1 x 14-oz can of light coconut milk

4 teaspoons tamarind paste

4 stalks of lemongrass

½ oz palm sugar

1–2 fresh red chilies

1½-inch piece of fresh ginger

7 oz mixed mushrooms

10 oz firm tofu

6 scallions

½ a bunch of fresh
    cilantro (½ oz)

reduced-sodium soy sauce

1 lime

Rub a large non-stick frying pan lightly with oil. Tip in the rice and twice the volume of water, season with a pinch of sea salt, then cover and cook on a high heat for 10 minutes. Remove the lid, then cook on a low heat for a further 5 minutes, or until the rice is fluffy with a crispy bottom, shaking the pan occasionally.

Meanwhile, tip the stock and coconut milk into a large pan, and add the tamarind paste. Peel the lemongrass and trim the ends, very finely chop the tender stalks and add to the pan, then roughly chop and add the palm sugar. Seed and finely slice the chili(es), peel and finely chop the ginger, then add it all to the pan and place over a medium heat. Roughly chop any larger mushrooms with the tofu, leaving any smaller ones whole, then add to the pan. Bring to a boil for a couple of minutes while you trim and finely slice the scallions and pick most of the cilantro leaves, then stir through with a drizzle of soy sauce, to taste.

Spoon the broth into bowls. Turn out the rice cake, slice into wedges and place on top. Serve with the remaining cilantro and lime wedges for squeezing over.

There's a lot of fun to be had here with seasonal veg and mushrooms – react to what's available and make the most of them.

ENERGY	FAT	SAT FAT	PROTEIN	CARBS	SUGARS	SALT	FIBER
384kcal	9g	4.4g	12.7g	65.9g	6g	0.4g	2.3g

MUSHROOM STROGANOFF

CRUNCHY CORNICHONS, FRAGRANT CAPERS, CREAMY WHISKY SAUCE & PARSLEY

SERVES 2 | 20 MINUTES

14 oz mixed mushrooms

1 red onion

2 cloves of garlic

4 silverskin pickled onions

2 cornichons

4 sprigs of fresh Italian parsley

olive oil

1 tablespoon baby capers

3 tablespoons whisky

smoked paprika

3 oz half-fat crème fraîche or
    sour cream

Get all the prep done before you start cooking: trim the mushrooms, tearing up any larger ones and leaving any smaller ones whole, peel and finely slice the red onion and garlic, and finely slice the pickled onions and cornichons. Pick and roughly chop the parsley leaves, finely chopping the stalks.

Place a large non-stick frying pan over a high heat, throw in the mushrooms and red onions, shake into one layer, then dry-fry for 5 minutes (this will bring out the nutty flavor), stirring regularly. Drizzle in 1 tablespoon of oil, then add the garlic, pickled onions, cornichons, parsley stalks and capers. After 3 minutes, pour in the whisky, tilt the pan to carefully flame, or light with a long match (watch your eyebrows!), and, once the flames subside, add ¼ of a teaspoon of paprika, the crème fraîche and parsley, then toss together. Loosen with a splash of boiling water to a saucy consistency, and season to taste with sea salt and black pepper.

Divide between plates, sprinkle over a little paprika and serve with fluffy rice.

Look out for seasonal wild mushrooms in supermarkets and local farmers' markets – they're absolutely extraordinary and will add so much bonus flavor to this dish.

ENERGY	FAT	SAT FAT	PROTEIN	CARBS	SUGARS	SALT	FIBER
251kcal	13.9g	5.2g	6.7g	11.9g	7.9g	0.8g	4.3g

WONDERFUL VEG TAGINE

SAFFRON, PRESERVED LEMONS, APRICOTS, FLUFFY COUSCOUS & TOASTED ALMONDS

SERVES 6 | 1 HOUR

1 pinch of saffron

4 cloves of garlic

1½-inch piece of fresh ginger

olive oil

1 teaspoon ground cumin

½ teaspoon ground cinnamon

1 teaspoon ras el hanout

1 tablespoon sun-dried
    tomato paste

5 lbs mixed veg, such as
    eggplants, zucchini, carrots,
    cherry tomatoes, red onion,
    butternut squash, mixed-color
    peppers

1 x 15-oz can of chickpeas

3½ oz dried apricots

1 preserved lemon

2 cups couscous

½ a bunch of mixed fresh
    herbs, such as dill, mint,
    Italian parsley (½ oz)

¾ oz flaked almonds

Put the saffron into a pitcher, cover with 2 cups of boiling water and leave to infuse. Meanwhile, peel and finely slice the garlic and ginger, then place in a large casserole pan over a medium heat with 2 tablespoons of oil, the cumin, cinnamon and ras el hanout. Add the tomato paste, fry for a few minutes, stirring regularly, then pour over the saffron water. Trim and prep the veg, as necessary, then chop into large chunks, adding them to the pan as you go. Tip in the chickpeas (juices and all), roughly chop and add the apricots and preserved lemon, discarding any pips, then season with sea salt and black pepper. Bring to a boil, cover, reduce the heat to low and simmer for 45 minutes, or until tender, stirring occasionally.

When the veg are almost tender, just cover the couscous with boiling water, season with salt and pepper and pop a plate on top. Leave for 10 minutes, then fluff and fork up. Pick the herb leaves and toast the almonds. Serve the tagine and couscous sprinkled with the almonds and herbs.

Delicious served with harissa rippled yogurt.

> In the summer I grow most of these vegetables, and I'm always eager to pick, wash and race to cook this dish — the flavor is just extraordinary with tender, delicate veg.

ENERGY	FAT	SAT FAT	PROTEIN	CARBS	SUGARS	SALT	FIBER
438kcal	9.6g	1.4g	16.3g	77.6g	27.7g	1g	15.8g

BREAD-TOPPED BIRYANI

CAULIFLOWER, CHICKPEA & GREEN BEAN CURRY, FRAGRANT SAFFRON RICE

SERVES 6 | 2 HOURS PLUS RESTING

2¼ cups basmati rice

2 cloves of garlic

1-inch piece of fresh ginger

2 onions

1 fresh red chili

3½ oz sun-dried tomato paste

1 bunch of fresh cilantro (1 oz)

3 cloves

1 cinnamon stick

olive oil

7 oz green beans

½ a head of cauliflower (14 oz)

2 x 12-oz jar of chickpeas

⅔ cup plain yogurt

1½ cups reduced-fat (2%) milk

1 good pinch of saffron

½ teaspoon cardamom pods

garam masala

1⅓ cups self-rising flour

Cook the rice in a large pan of boiling salted water for exactly 7 minutes, then drain and spread out on a tray to cool. Meanwhile, peel and roughly chop the garlic, ginger and onions. Whiz to a paste in a blender with the chili, tomato paste, most of the cilantro and a splash of water. Put the cloves and cinnamon into a large pan on a medium heat with 2 tablespoons of oil and fry for 2 minutes, then tip in the paste and cook for 10 minutes, stirring regularly. Trim and halve the beans and break the cauliflower into bite-sized florets, then add to the pan with the chickpeas (juices and all). Stir in the yogurt, cover and simmer on a low heat for 10 minutes, then season to perfection with sea salt and black pepper.

Preheat the oven to 350°F. Gently heat the milk over a low heat until warm, then turn the heat off. Add the saffron, bash and add the cardamom pods, then leave to infuse. Lightly oil a 9-inch springform cake pan and place on a baking sheet. Spoon in a third of the rice and really press down to compact. Drizzle over ¼ cup of the saffron milk, dust with 1 teaspoon of garam masala and spoon over half the curry. Repeat the layers once more, pressing as you go and finishing with a top layer of rice and 4 more tablespoons of the saffron milk.

Add the flour to the remaining saffron milk and bring together into a dough (add extra flour, if needed). Knead until smooth, then roll out so it's just bigger than the pan. Place on top, pressing the edges to seal. Rub with oil, dust with garam masala and bake at the bottom of the oven for 40 minutes, or until golden. Rest for 15 minutes, then remove the bread lid and tear into portions, release from the pan, and pick, finely chop and scatter over the remaining cilantro. Always good served with a squeeze of lemon, a green salad and a dollop of yogurt.

ENERGY	FAT	SAT FAT	PROTEIN	CARBS	SUGARS	SALT	FIBER
699kcal	17.4g	3.6g	23.1g	116.1g	12.8g	1.6g	10.4g

PIES, PARCELS
& BAKES

ALLOTMENT COTTAGE PIE

ROOT VEG, PORCINI MUSHROOMS, MARMITE & CRISPY ROSEMARY

SERVES 6-8 | 2 HOURS

⅓ oz dried porcini mushrooms

2 large leeks

3 carrots

1 lb rutabaga

1 lb celery root

olive oil

3 sprigs of fresh rosemary

1 teaspoon cumin seeds

4½ lbs potatoes

3 tablespoons unsalted butter

1 splash of reduced-fat (2%) milk

1 onion

1 teaspoon Marmite

3 tablespoons tomato paste

1 x 15-oz can of green lentils

Preheat the oven to 375°F. In a blender, cover the porcini with 2½ cups of boiling water. Trim, wash and slice the leeks ¾ inch thick, then scrub the carrots, rutabaga and celery root and chop to roughly the same size. Drizzle 2 tablespoons of oil into a large casserole pan on a medium heat, strip in the rosemary, fry for 1 minute to crisp up, then remove to a plate with a slotted spoon. Add the cumin seeds and prepped veg to the flavored oil, season with sea salt and black pepper, and cook for 30 minutes, stirring regularly.

Meanwhile, peel and roughly chop the potatoes, cook in a pan of boiling salted water for 15 minutes, or until tender, then drain well. Mash with the butter and milk, and season to taste. Quarter the onion, add to the porcini in the blender along with the Marmite and tomato paste and whiz until smooth. Pour into the veg pan and cook for 20 minutes, or until dark and caramelized, stirring regularly and scraping up any sticky bits from the bottom of the pan.

Tip the lentils (juices and all) into the veg pan, bring to a boil, then season to taste. Spoon over the mash, place on a baking sheet, bake for 30 minutes, or until lightly golden and bubbling at the edges, then sprinkle over the crispy rosemary.

Serve with simple steamed seasonal greens – it's a winner!

Sometimes I swap the lentils for borlotti or lima beans – both work really well.

ENERGY	FAT	SAT FAT	PROTEIN	CARBS	SUGARS	SALT	FIBER
466kcal	12g	4.4g	14g	80g	15g	0.8g	13.7g

STICKY ONION TART

SWEET GARLIC, FRESH THYME, BAY & BUTTERY PUFF PASTRY

SERVES 6 | 50 MINUTES

4 medium onions

¼ cup unsalted butter

4 sprigs of fresh thyme

4 fresh bay leaves

2 tablespoons soft dark
brown sugar

¼ cup cider vinegar

8 cloves of garlic

11-oz sheet of all-butter puff
pastry (cold)

Preheat the oven to 425°F. Peel the onions and halve across the middle. Place the butter in a 10-inch non-stick ovenproof frying pan on a medium heat. Strip in the thyme leaves and add the bay, shake the pan around and get it bubbling, then add the sugar, vinegar and 6 tablespoons of water. Place the onion halves in the pan, cut-side down. Peel and halve the garlic cloves and place in the gaps, then season generously with sea salt and black pepper. Cover, turn the heat down to low and leave to steam for 10 minutes to soften the onions slightly, then remove the lid and cook until – very importantly! – the liquid starts to caramelize, gently shaking the pan occasionally to stop it from sticking.

Place the pastry over the onions, using a wooden spoon to push it right into the edges of the pan. Bake for 35 minutes, or until golden brown and puffed up (it will look quite dark, but don't worry!). Using oven gloves to protect your hands, pop a large plate over the pan and confidently but very carefully turn out.

Delicious served with goat's cheese, a simple salad and a cold beer.

Shallots, leeks and scallions all make wonderful tarts – just make sure they're soft and caramelized before covering with pastry.

ENERGY	FAT	SAT FAT	PROTEIN	CARBS	SUGARS	SALT	FIBER
352kcal	21.6g	13.6g	4.4g	35.3g	13.5g	0.6g	3.5g

ROASTED VEG DOSA

TOMATO & GINGER SALSA, FRESHLY GRATED COCONUT

SERVES 6 | 1 HOUR 45 MINUTES PLUS SOAKING & FERMENTING

¾ cup white urid dal
(split white gram)

1½ cups basmati rice

2 tablespoons fenugreek seeds

2 red onions

2 peppers

2 potatoes

2 sweet potatoes (8 oz each)

olive oil

2 oz freshly grated coconut

2-inch piece of fresh ginger

12 ripe cherry tomatoes

2 cloves of garlic

2 fresh red chilies

2 teaspoons cumin seeds

2 teaspoons mustard seeds

1 knob of unsalted butter

½ a bunch of fresh cilantro (½ oz)

Thoroughly wash the dal, rice and fenugreek, then drain and place in a blender. Top up with 3⅔ cups of fresh water and leave for 6 hours with the lid on to soak (transfer to a covered bowl and work in batches if you have a small blender), then blitz. Leave overnight at room temperature to ferment, then blitz again until super-smooth – this batter will be good for 2 days in the fridge. When you're ready to cook, preheat the oven to 350°F. Rub the onions, peppers, potatoes and sweet potatoes with 1 tablespoon of oil, then place in a snug-fitting roasting pan. Roast with a splash of water for 1 hour, or until soft, then remove.

Meanwhile, place the coconut in a small bowl. Peel the ginger, then finely grate just ½ inch with the tomatoes and scrape into a second bowl, seasoning with sea salt and black pepper. Peel the garlic, then finely chop with the remaining ginger and the chilies. Gently fry the cumin and mustard seeds in a large non-stick frying pan on a medium heat with the butter for 1 minute. Add the garlic, ginger and chilies, fry for 1 minute, then tear in all the roast vegetables, discarding any tough skins and seeds, and saving any juices from the pan, to serve. Mix and mash everything together, season to perfection with salt and pepper, pick in the cilantro leaves and fry until golden. Keep warm while you make the dosas.

Place a large non-stick frying pan over a medium heat, pour in a ladle of batter and swirl around to create a thin layer. Cook for 5 minutes, or until crispy and golden on just one side, then roll up and repeat. Serve with the veg, dips and sprinkles.

Mango chutney folded through the roasting juices is always a nice addition.

ENERGY	FAT	SAT FAT	PROTEIN	CARBS	SUGARS	SALT	FIBER
480kcal	10.7g	5.8g	15.6g	87.6g	12.8g	0.5g	4.9g

SUMMER VEG BLANKET PIE

PRESERVED LEMON, SAFFRON, HARISSA, CRISPY LAYERED PHYLLO, YOGURT

SERVES 4 | 1 HOUR 30 MINUTES

1½ cups plain yogurt

11 oz ripe cherry tomatoes

extra virgin olive oil

1 tablespoon red wine vinegar

4 cloves of garlic

1 tablespoon fennel seeds

olive oil

1 large leek

11 oz new potatoes

11 oz butternut squash

11 oz zucchini

1 x 12-oz jar of chickpeas

1 preserved lemon

1 teaspoon rose harissa

1¾ oz dried sour cherries

1 pinch of saffron

8 sheets of phyllo pastry

1 tablespoon sesame seeds

Line a sieve with 3 pieces of paper towel, tip in the yogurt, pull up the paper and very gently apply pressure so that the liquid starts to drip through into a bowl, then leave to drain. Halve the tomatoes, season with sea salt and black pepper, drizzle with 2 tablespoons of extra virgin olive oil and the vinegar, then toss and leave to macerate (this really brings out the flavor).

Preheat the oven to 375°F. Peel and finely slice the garlic, then place in a large non-stick ovenproof frying pan on a medium heat with the fennel seeds and 2 tablespoons of olive oil. Fry for a few minutes, stirring regularly, while you prep the veg, adding to the pan as you go: trim, wash and slice the leek, scrub the potatoes, squash (seed, if needed) and zucchini and chop into ¾-inch chunks. Cover and cook for 15 minutes, shaking the pan occasionally, then remove the lid, tip in the chickpeas (juices and all) and season lightly with a pinch of salt and pepper. Finely chop the preserved lemon, discarding any pips, then add to the pan with a drizzle of juice from the jar, and the harissa. Fry for a further 15 minutes, or until beautifully caramelized, stirring occasionally.

Meanwhile, cover the sour cherries and saffron with 1¼ cups of boiling water, leave for a few minutes, then add to the pan with the tomatoes, reserving the macerating juices. Lay the phyllo out flat, then brush all over with the reserved tomato juices. Roughly scrunch, wave and layer the phyllo into the pan, partly tucking it in at the edges (there's no need to be neat). Scatter over the sesame seeds and bake for 25 minutes, or until golden and crisp. Transfer the yogurt to a plate and drizzle with a little oil from the harissa jar, then serve with the pie.

ENERGY	FAT	SAT FAT	PROTEIN	CARBS	SUGARS	SALT	FIBER
641kcal	23.7g	5.6g	20.5g	90.6g	28.8g	1.7g	9.4g

CAULIFLOWER CHEESE PIZZA PIE

OOZY MELTY CHEESY WHITE SAUCE, SUPER-CRISPY CRUST

SERVES 4–6 | 1 HOUR 10 MINUTES PLUS PROVING

1 x ¼-oz package of dried yeast

3⅔ cups bread flour, plus extra
for dusting

olive oil

1 onion

¼ cup unsalted butter

4 fresh bay leaves

2 teaspoons English mustard

3 cups reduced-fat (2%) milk

1 small head of cauliflower,
ideally with leaves (1¼ lbs)

4 oz sharp Cheddar cheese

Whisk the yeast into 1¼ cups of lukewarm water, leave for 2 minutes, then pour into a large bowl with 3⅓ cups of the flour and a really good pinch of sea salt. Mix up as best you can, then knead vigorously on a flour-dusted surface to give you a smooth, elastic dough. Rub lightly with oil, place in the bowl, cover with a clean damp kitchen towel and proof for 1 hour in a warm place, or until doubled in size.

Meanwhile, peel and finely slice the onion and place in a pan with the butter, bay leaves and a splash of water. Fry on a medium heat for 10 minutes, stirring regularly, then stir in ⅓ cup of flour, followed by the mustard, and slowly add the milk to give you a loose white sauce. Roughly break up the cauliflower, discarding just the tatty outer leaves, and finely slice the stalk. Add to the pan with any remaining leaves. Simmer gently for 30 minutes, stirring occasionally, then turn off the heat, grate in the cheese, season to perfection and allow to cool a little.

Preheat the oven to full whack (475°F). Lightly oil a 12-inch non-stick ovenproof frying pan or a 14- x 10-inch baking pan, then press out the dough to fill the space. Spoon over the cauliflower mixture, leaving a ¾-inch border around the edge, then leave to proof again until doubled in size. Bake at the bottom of the oven for 25 minutes, or until golden, crisp and melty.

Delicious served with a bowl of lemony dressed seasonal salad leaves.

> Mix up the cheeses you choose — also incredible made
> with broccoli instead of, or as well as, the cauliflower.

ENERGY	FAT	SAT FAT	PROTEIN	CARBS	SUGARS	SALT	FIBER
876kcal	28.5g	15.9g	34.6g	128.6g	17.1g	1.5g	8.2g

CRISPY-BOTTOMED STEAMED DUMPLINGS

ROASTED SQUASH, BROCCOLI, GARLIC, GINGER, MISO, CHILI & SESAME SEEDS

SERVES 4 | 1 HOUR 35 MINUTES PLUS COOLING

1 lb butternut squash

olive oil

1 clove of garlic

2½-inch piece of fresh ginger

3 oz broccoli

1 teaspoon red miso paste

1 tablespoon rice wine vinegar

24 x 4-inch square wonton wrappers

½ a fresh red chili

2 scallions

2 tablespoons sesame seeds

reduced-sodium soy sauce

English mustard

1 lime

Preheat the oven to 350°F. Quarter the squash, seed and toss with 1 tablespoon of oil and a pinch of sea salt and black pepper, then roast on a baking sheet for 1 hour, or until soft and golden. Leave to cool.

Peel the garlic and ¾ inch of the ginger, then whiz in a food processor with the broccoli, miso and vinegar until fine. Pulse in the squash, then season to taste.

One by one, lightly wet the edges of the wonton wrappers with your finger, add 1 heaping teaspoon of filling to the middle of each, and pinch together to seal (don't stress if they tear every now and again), placing them in a large oiled non-stick frying pan as you go. Put the pan over a high heat, then pour over ⅔ cup of water and cover. Let it steam until the water has completely evaporated, then uncover and allow to fry, removing as soon as the bottoms are golden and crisp.

Meanwhile, peel the remaining ginger, finely grate with the chili, and place in a small dipping bowl. Trim and finely shred the scallions, toast the sesame seeds, then serve with soy, mustard and lime wedges.

> I love swapping in sweet peas, asparagus, water chestnuts and edamame – delicious!

ENERGY	FAT	SAT FAT	PROTEIN	CARBS	SUGARS	SALT	FIBER
227kcal	7g	1.1g	6.9g	33.7g	6.7g	1.2g	4.1g

ASPARAGUS QUICHE & SOUP

WHOLE-WHEAT PASTRY, THYME, RICOTTA & CHEDDAR

SERVES 8 | 1 HOUR 15 MINUTES PLUS CHILLING

heaping ¾ cup all-purpose flour

heaping ¾ cup whole-wheat flour

9 tablespoons unsalted butter (cold)

7 large eggs

2 lbs asparagus

olive oil

2 large potatoes

2 onions

½ a bunch of fresh thyme (½ oz)

6 cups vegetable stock

5 oz ricotta cheese

5 oz sharp Cheddar cheese

Preheat the oven to 350°F. Tip the flours into a bowl with a good pinch of sea salt, then chop and rub in the butter. Make a well in the middle, crack in one of the eggs, add 2 tablespoons of cold water, then mix, pat and bring together. Place between two large sheets of parchment paper, flatten to ¾ inch thick and chill in the fridge for 30 minutes. Roll out the pastry between the sheets of parchment, then line a 10-inch loose-bottomed tart pan with the pastry, easing and pushing it carefully into the sides and letting the pastry scruffily hang right over the sides (this will stop it shrinking). Prick the base all over with a fork and bake for 20 minutes, or until lightly golden, then trim off the excess pastry (sometimes I don't bother as people seem to love the crispy bits).

Halve the asparagus spears, saving the tips for the quiche. Chop and place the rest in a large pan over a medium heat with 1 tablespoon of oil. Peel, roughly chop and add the potatoes and onions and strip in half the thyme leaves, and cook for 15 minutes, or until lightly golden, stirring regularly. Pour in the stock, bring to a boil, then simmer for 15 minutes. Whiz with an immersion blender until smooth, pass through a sieve, then season to taste with salt and black pepper.

While the soup is on the go, beat the remaining eggs in a bowl with a pinch of salt and pepper and the ricotta, then grate in the Cheddar and pick in the remaining thyme leaves. Chop and add the reserved asparagus tips, then stir into the egg mixture and tip into the tart case. Bake for 40 minutes, or until beautifully golden. I like to serve the quiche and soup together – it's a wonderful meal.

ENERGY	FAT	SAT FAT	PROTEIN	CARBS	SUGARS	SALT	FIBER
514kcal	30.4g	15.4g	23.1g	39.7g	6.3g	1.1g	5.5g

MY VEGGIE MOUSSAKA

SWEET TOMATO, GRILLED EGGPLANTS, CREAMY PORCINI & FETA SAUCE

SERVES 8 | 2 HOURS

1½ oz dried porcini mushrooms

2 onions

8 cloves of garlic

olive oil

½ a cinnamon stick

1 bunch of fresh oregano (1 oz)

2 tablespoons red wine vinegar

2 large eggplants (14 oz each)

2 lbs potatoes

2 x 15-oz cans of quality plum
    tomatoes

7 oz feta cheese

2 large eggs

2 cups reduced-fat (2%) milk

1 whole nutmeg, for grating

Cover the porcini with 2 cups of boiling water. Peel and finely slice the onions and garlic. Drizzle 2 tablespoons of oil into a large casserole pan over a medium-low heat, add the cinnamon and fry for 1 minute, then add the onions and garlic. Pick in the oregano leaves, pour in the vinegar, then simmer with the lid on for 20 minutes, or until soft and lightly golden, stirring regularly. Meanwhile, slice the eggplants lengthways ½ inch thick, then chargrill in batches on a grill pan.

Scrub the potatoes and slice ½ inch thick, then add to the casserole pan with just the porcini water, reserving the mushrooms. Scrunch the tomatoes into the pan, then pour in 1 can's worth of water and leave to tick away on a medium heat for 30 minutes, stirring regularly. Preheat the oven to 400°F.

Place the mushrooms in a blender with half the feta and the eggs. Pour in the milk, finely grate in half the nutmeg, then whiz until smooth. Season the tomato sauce to perfection with sea salt and black pepper, then spoon half into a 14- x 10-inch baking dish. Cover with half the eggplants, drizzle over ¼ cup of creamy sauce, then repeat, finishing with the remaining creamy sauce. Crumble over the rest of the feta, then bake for 40 minutes, or until golden and bubbling.

Delicious served with a simple lemony dressed green salad.

> Sometimes I swap the feta for grated halloumi. Ribbons of zucchini grilled with the eggplant are very nice, too.

ENERGY	FAT	SAT FAT	PROTEIN	CARBS	SUGARS	SALT	FIBER
311kcal	11.6g	5.2g	14.6g	40g	13.4g	0.8g	5.6g

PITHIVIER PIE

GOLDEN PASTRY, CELERY ROOT, CREAMY LEEK, MUSHROOM & BLUE CHEESE SAUCE

SERVES 10 | 4 HOURS 30 MINUTES PLUS OVERNIGHT CHILLING

1 whole celery root (2 lbs)

olive oil

2 large leeks

1 knob of unsalted butter

2 cloves of garlic

14 oz mixed mushrooms

½ cup all-purpose flour

2 teaspoons English mustard

3¼ cups reduced-fat (2%) milk

1 bunch of fresh Italian
parsley (1 oz)

4 oz blue cheese

2 x 11-oz sheets of all-butter
puff pastry (cold)

1 large egg

Preheat the oven to 400°F. Scrub the celery root, rub with 1 tablespoon of oil and wrap in aluminum foil. Roast for 1 hour 30 minutes, then finely slice and season with sea salt and black pepper. Meanwhile, halve, wash and finely slice the leeks, then place in a large casserole pan on a medium heat with the butter. Peel, finely slice and add the garlic and mushrooms, then cook for 15 minutes. Stir in the flour and mustard, followed slowly by the milk, then simmer for 5 minutes, or until thickened, stirring regularly, and remove from the heat. Pick, finely chop and stir in the parsley, crumble in the cheese, then season to perfection.

Line a 8-inch bowl (3¼ inches deep) with plastic wrap. Arrange slices of celery root in and around the bowl until covered. Reserving half the sauce, layer up the rest with the remaining celery root in the bowl, finishing with celery root. Pull over the plastic wrap, weigh it down with something heavy, and chill overnight with the remaining sauce.

Preheat the oven to 350°F. On parchment paper, roll both sheets of pastry out to around 14 x 12 inches. Unwrap the filling parcel and place in the middle of one sheet. Beat the egg and brush around the edge of the pastry and all over the celery root, then carefully lay the second piece of pastry on top, smoothing around the shape of the filling. Trim the edges to 1 inch, crimp to seal, then eggwash all over. Very lightly score the pastry (like in the picture), making a small hole in the top. Bake at the bottom of the oven for 2 hours, or until beautifully golden, brushing with more eggwash once or twice, then serve with the warmed-up creamy sauce. Delicious with dressed seasonal steamed greens.

ENERGY	FAT	SAT FAT	PROTEIN	CARBS	SUGARS	SALT	FIBER
442kcal	27.4g	16.2g	12.8g	36.2g	7.6g	1g	6.2g

PHYLLO SNAKE BAKE

SPINACH, OLIVE & FETA FILLING, LETTUCE & BLOOD ORANGE SALAD BITES

SERVES 6 | 1 HOUR 45 MINUTES PLUS COOLING

1 onion

4 cloves of garlic

olive oil

10 black olives (with pits)

1 bunch of fresh oregano (1 oz)

1 lb baby spinach

1 x 9-oz jar of roasted red peppers in brine

5 oz artichoke hearts in oil

2 tablespoons couscous

6 sheets of phyllo pastry

3½ oz feta cheese

2 large eggs

3 little gem lettuces

3 regular or blood oranges

Peel and finely slice the onion and garlic, then place in a large casserole pan over a medium heat with 2 tablespoons of oil. Pit and tear in the olives and pick in the oregano leaves, then fry for 5 minutes, stirring regularly. Add the spinach and tear in the peppers and artichokes, then fry for a further 10 minutes, or until all of the juices have cooked away. Season to taste with sea salt and black pepper, then stir in the couscous and leave aside to cool.

Preheat the oven to 375°F. Lay out 3 sheets of phyllo side by side on an oiled work surface, overlapping each one and brushing between the overlaps with water to create one long sheet, then rub lightly all over with oil. Lay the remaining sheets on top in the same way to create a double layer. Crumble the feta into the spinach mixture, beat and mix in the eggs, then spoon evenly along the bottom edge. Roll up into a long snake (be confident and don't worry about cracks and tears – it cooks into a beautiful thing), then slowly and loosely wind up like a Catherine wheel. Quickly and carefully slide onto a lightly oiled baking sheet, and bake at the bottom of the oven for 50 minutes, or until golden and crisp.

Trim and click apart the lettuce leaves, peel and segment the oranges, then buddy up and serve alongside the phyllo bake. Bloomin' delicious!

> As well as spinach in this dish, it's really nice to use different greens, such as chard, dandelions, stinging nettles, watercress or arugula, soft herbs, or even edible flowers.

ENERGY	FAT	SAT FAT	PROTEIN	CARBS	SUGARS	SALT	FIBER
388kcal	17.9g	4.5g	14g	44g	13.4g	2.1g	6.2g

MY VEGGIE PASTIES

MIXED MUSHROOMS, RUTABAGA, POTATO, ONION, ROSEMARY

MAKES 8 | I HOUR 45 MINUTES PLUS CHILLING

1 lb mixed mushrooms

3⅓ cups bread flour, plus extra
for dusting

1 cup + 1 tablespoon unsalted
butter (cold)

7 oz rutabaga

14 oz potatoes

1 onion

1 pinch of dried rosemary

1 large egg

Tear the mushrooms into a bowl, scatter over ½ oz of sea salt (most of this will drain away later) and scrunch together, then leave for 30 minutes, scrunching occasionally. Tip the flour into a bowl with a pinch of salt, then chop and rub in the butter. Make a well in the middle, slowly pour in ¾ cup + 5 teaspoons of cold water, then mix, pat and bring it together. Wrap in plastic wrap and chill in the fridge for 1 hour.

After 30 minutes the mushrooms should feel quite soggy, so squeeze firmly to remove as much salty liquid as you can (the mushrooms should end up weighing around 14 oz). Peel the rutabaga, potatoes and onion and slice into small rounds, roughly ⅛ inch thick. Mix the veg with the mushrooms, then add the rosemary and a few generous pinches of black pepper.

Preheat the oven to 350°F. Divide the pastry into 8, then roll out into 8-inch rounds on a clean flour-dusted surface. Divide up the filling, then scrunch and pile it to one side of the middle, leaving a 1-inch gap around the edges. Lightly brush the exposed pastry with beaten egg, fold over and press the edges down, then twist and crimp with your fingers and thumbs to seal. Eggwash, then place on a lined baking sheet and bake for 40 minutes, or until golden.

Serve with a watercress and apple salad and a dollop of English mustard.

These freeze really well raw – simply bake to order straight from frozen at 350°F for 1 hour.

ENERGY	FAT	SAT FAT	PROTEIN	CARBS	SUGARS	SALT	FIBER
516kcal	27.8g	16.6g	9.6g	60.8g	4g	1.1g	4g

YEMENI-STYLE PANCAKES

SMOKY EGGPLANT, CREAMY TAHINI, FRESH SALSAS

SERVES 4 | 45 MINUTES

2 cups bread flour

1 x ¼-oz package of dried yeast

2 large eggplants (14 oz each)

1 clove of garlic

2 lemons

¼ cup plain yogurt

2 tablespoons tahini

4 sprigs of fresh cilantro

1 big bunch of fresh Italian
    parsley (2 oz)

2 fresh green chilies

extra virgin olive oil

4 ripe tomatoes

olive oil

4 large eggs

Tip the flour into a bowl, add a pinch of sea salt and the yeast, then whisk in 2 cups of lukewarm water and leave aside for 30 minutes to do its thing – it should be aerated and bubbly. Meanwhile, place the eggplants directly over the flame of a gas stove or on a grill pan, until soft and blackened all over, turning with tongs. Slice the eggplants open, transfer to a plate, then peel and finely grate over the garlic, season with salt and add a squeeze of lemon juice. Spoon over the yogurt and tahini, pick over the cilantro leaves, then leave aside.

Pick most of the parsley and very finely chop with the chilies (seed, if you like), then scrape into a bowl and stir in 2 tablespoons of extra virgin olive oil and the juice of 1 lemon. Grate the tomatoes onto a plate, discarding any skins, then season to taste with salt, black pepper and lemon juice.

When you're ready to cook, place a medium non-stick frying pan on a medium heat with 1 teaspoon of olive oil. Once hot, add a ladle of batter, tilting to spread it up and around the edges. Cook until it dries up and starts to come away from the sides, then crack an egg on top and use a fork to break and spread it over the surface of the pancake. Pick over a few parsley leaves and fold over, then turn regularly until golden on both sides, clank up and repeat. To serve, spoon over the fresh salsas and scoop over the tahini eggplant (leaving the blackened skin behind). Cut any remaining lemon into wedges for squeezing over.

If you're feeding a crowd, get all the pancakes made and stacked up in advance, then simply reheat, cooking the eggs at the same time.

ENERGY	FAT	SAT FAT	PROTEIN	CARBS	SUGARS	SALT	FIBER
513kcal	20.4g	4.2g	21.7g	65.8g	9.6g	0.8g	7.2g

EASY PEA & SPINACH SAMOSAS

YOGURT, MANGO & CHILI RIPPLE

SERVES 8 (MAKES 16) | 1 HOUR 15 MINUTES PLUS COOLING

1 carrot

1 onion

olive oil

2 cloves of garlic

2-inch piece of fresh ginger

1 tablespoon rogan josh curry paste

1 x 15-oz can of chickpeas

3½ oz frozen peas

3½ oz baby spinach

1 bunch of fresh mint (1 oz)

3½ oz paneer cheese

4 sheets of phyllo pastry

1 tablespoon sesame seeds

½ a ripe mango

1 lime

1¼ cups plain yogurt

chili oil

Peel the carrot and onion, chop into ½-inch cubes, then place in a large non-stick frying pan on a medium heat with 1 tablespoon of olive oil. Peel, finely chop and add the garlic and ginger, then cook on low for 20 minutes, stirring regularly. Add the curry paste and fry for 1 minute. Tip in the chickpeas (juices and all), peas and spinach, and cook for 10 minutes, or until the juices have evaporated. Roughly mash and season to perfection with sea salt and black pepper. Pick the mint leaves, then finely chop with the paneer and stir through. Leave to cool.

Preheat the oven to 400°F. Lay a clean damp kitchen towel out flat on a work surface, then place a sheet of phyllo on top and cut into 4 strips. Brush the edges of each strip lightly with water, then spoon 1 heaping tablespoon of filling into the bottom corner of each. Fold diagonally up to create triangle shapes, then roll and fold up the samosas, tucking in the sides and pressing lightly to seal as you go (it doesn't matter if they're a bit untidy – you'll get better as you go), and repeat. Brush with olive oil and sprinkle with sesame seeds, dividing them between oiled baking sheets. Bake for 20 minutes, or until golden and crisp.

Peel and pit the mango, then whiz in a blender with the lime juice. Ripple with the yogurt and a little chili oil, to taste.

Nice served hot, or even cold as part of a packed lunch with a salad.

> Sometimes I like to sprinkle the phyllo with garam masala before rolling up for an extra kick – super-tasty!

ENERGY	FAT	SAT FAT	PROTEIN	CARBS	SUGARS	SALT	FIBER
245kcal	11.1g	3.6g	10.9g	26.6g	8.2g	0.4g	4.1g

SOUPS & SANDWICHES

SPICED PARSNIP SOUP

SILKY PAPPADAMS & FUNKY CRISPS

SERVES 4 | 50 MINUTES

1¾ lbs parsnips

1 onion

2 cloves of garlic

2-inch piece of fresh ginger

olive oil

1 teaspoon cumin seeds

garam masala

7 oz red split lentils

4 uncooked pappadams

6 cups vegetable stock

¼ cup plain yogurt

4 sprigs of fresh cilantro

optional: chili oil

Preheat the oven to 350°F. Put 2 parsnips aside for later. Peel the onion, roughly chop with the remaining parsnips (keep the skins on) and peel and finely grate the garlic and ginger. Place the parsnips and onions in a large pan over a medium heat with 1 tablespoon of olive oil, then cover and cook for 20 minutes, or until dark golden, stirring occasionally. Add the garlic and ginger, then scatter over the cumin seeds, 1 teaspoon of garam masala and the lentils and cook for a further 5 minutes. Roughly snap in the uncooked pappadams, then add the stock and simmer for 20 minutes, loosening with a splash of water, if needed.

Meanwhile, peel the reserved parsnips into ribbons until you reach the woody core (discard this bit), blanch for 30 seconds in fast-boiling water, then drain and pat dry. Season with sea salt, then spread out in a single layer over a couple of oiled baking sheets. Roast for 15 minutes, or until golden and crisp. Season the soup to perfection, ripple through the yogurt and divide between warm bowls. Pick over the cilantro leaves, sprinkle with a little garam masala, and top with the parsnip crisps. Feel free to drizzle with chili oil for a warm glow.

> You can make this soup as chunky or as smooth as you like, and if you cook it a little drier, it makes a fantastic side dish as part of a bigger curry feast.

ENERGY	FAT	SAT FAT	PROTEIN	CARBS	SUGARS	SALT	FIBER
428kcal	11.7g	2g	21.6g	62.2g	16.9g	1.1g	11.3g

CRISPY MUSHROOM SHAWARMA

TAHINI FLATBREADS, PICKLES, MINTED JALAPEÑO SALSA & DUKKAH

SERVES 4 | 1 HOUR PLUS MARINATING

¾ cup plain yogurt

1¾ lbs portobello and oyster
mushrooms

1 red onion

2 cloves of garlic

2 preserved lemons

1 teaspoon each ground
cumin, ground allspice,
smoked paprika

olive oil

2 tablespoons pomegranate
molasses

10 radishes, ideally with leaves

½ an English cucumber

3½ oz ripe cherry tomatoes

1 tablespoon white wine vinegar

1 x 7-oz jar of pickled jalapeño
chilies

1 bunch of fresh mint (1 oz)

4 large flatbreads

¼ cup tahini

2 tablespoons dukkah

Line a sieve with pieces of paper towel, tip in the yogurt and pull up the paper and very gently apply pressure so that the liquid starts to drip through into a bowl, then leave to drain. Peel and trim just the portobello mushrooms, then peel and quarter the onion and separate into petals. Peel the garlic, roughly chop the preserved lemons, discarding any pips, and bash to a paste in a pestle and mortar with ½ a teaspoon of sea salt, 1 teaspoon of black pepper and the spices. Muddle in 1 tablespoon of oil, then toss with all the mushrooms and onions. Marinate for at least 2 hours, preferably overnight.

When you're ready to cook, preheat the oven to full whack (475°F). Randomly thread the mushrooms and onions onto a large skewer, then place on a large baking sheet and roast for 20 minutes, turning occasionally. Push the veg together so it's all snug, baste with any juices from the pan, then roast for a further 15 minutes, or until gnarly, drizzling over the pomegranate molasses for the last 3 minutes. Meanwhile, finely slice the radishes and cucumber, ideally on a mandolin (use the guard!), and quarter the tomatoes, toss with a pinch of salt and the vinegar, then leave aside. Tip the jalapeños (juices and all) into a blender, then pick in most of the mint leaves and whiz until fine. Pour back into the jar — this will keep in the fridge for a couple of weeks for jazzing up future meals.

Warm the flatbreads, spread with tahini, then sprinkle over the pickled veg, remaining mint leaves and dukkah. Carve and scatter over the gnarly veg, dollop over the drained yogurt, drizzle with jalapeño salsa, then roll up, slice and tuck in.

> If you find the tahini has separated in the jar, add
> a splash of hot water and mix until spoonable.

ENERGY	FAT	SAT FAT	PROTEIN	CARBS	SUGARS	SALT	FIBER
357kcal	18.2g	3.5g	14.3g	33.3g	13.6g	1.8g	5.7g

BOLD BLACK BEAN SOUP

JAZZED UP WITH LIME-SPIKED AVOCADO, FETA & CHILI

SERVES 2 | **30 MINUTES**

2 red onions

2 cloves of garlic

2 stalks of celery

1 fresh red chili

olive oil

1 teaspoon cumin seeds

1 x 15-oz can of black beans

1 ripe avocado

1 lime

¾ oz feta cheese

optional: 2 sprigs of fresh cilantro

extra virgin olive oil

Peel the onions and garlic, then finely chop with the celery and chili, reserving a little chili for garnish. Place in a large pan on a medium heat with 1 tablespoon of olive oil and the cumin seeds. Cook for 15 minutes, stirring regularly, then tip in the black beans (juices and all) and 1 can's worth of water. Simmer for 15 minutes, or until thickened and reduced, then spoon out a ladle's worth. Whiz the rest of the soup with an immersion blender (or in a regular blender) until smooth and thick, and season to perfection with sea salt and black pepper. Peel, pit and slice the avocado, season with salt and squeeze over half the lime juice.

Divide the smooth soup between warm bowls, and top with the reserved chunky soup and avocado. Crumble over the feta and sprinkle with the reserved chili. Pick over the cilantro leaves (if using), drizzle with a little extra virgin olive oil and serve with lime wedges for squeezing over.

> This makes a strangely perfect weekend brunch served with a wodge of sourdough bread at the bottom of the bowl and a perfectly poached egg on top. Hurrah!

ENERGY	FAT	SAT FAT	PROTEIN	CARBS	SUGARS	SALT	FIBER
371kcal	21.7g	4.9g	13.8g	25.5g	12g	0.9g	15.6g

SUPER STACKED SARNIE

GRILLED MEDITERRANEAN VEGETABLES, FRESH MINT DRESSING & BLACK OLIVES

SERVES 8 | 45 MINUTES PLUS PRESSING

2 large ripe tomatoes

2 mixed-color peppers

2 mixed-color zucchini

½ a head of cauliflower (14 oz)

2 red onions

1 bunch of fresh mint (1 oz)

extra virgin olive oil

2 tablespoons red wine vinegar

8 black olives (with pits)

1 large loaf of crusty rustic bread (2 lbs)

4½-oz ball of mozzarella cheese

Preheat a grill pan to high. Halve the tomatoes, seed the peppers and tear into chunks, slice up the zucchini and cauliflower, and peel and quarter the onions. Working in batches, grill all the veg until charred, transferring to a bowl as you go. Pick the mint leaves into a pestle and mortar, pound to a paste, then muddle in ¼ cup of oil and the vinegar. Pit the olives, add to the bowl with the dressing and toss to coat. Season with sea salt and black pepper.

Slice the top off the loaf. Pull out the soft insides to hollow out the bread – do it as evenly as you can and get right into the edges (use whatever you pull out to make flavored breadcrumbs for another day – see page 280).

Slice up the mozzarella and toss with the dressed veg, then put it all into the hollowed-out bread, compacting and pushing it all into the edges. Pop the top of the bread back on, then press down really hard to compress. Wrap in plastic wrap, then place in the fridge with something heavy on top and leave for at least 4 hours, preferably longer. Remove from the fridge 20 minutes before you want to eat it, slice into wedges and tuck in.

> I've used a 2-lb loaf here, but use two smaller loaves if these are easier for you to find.

ENERGY	FAT	SAT FAT	PROTEIN	CARBS	SUGARS	SALT	FIBER
489kcal	16.8g	4.2g	16.4g	72.4g	8.9g	1.3g	7.3g

SILKY FENNEL SOUP

VIBRANT SPINACH SWIRL, CHUNKY PARMESAN CROUTONS

SERVES 4 | 40 MINUTES

2 bulbs of fennel

2 onions

10 oz potatoes

olive oil

4 slices of rustic bread

¾ oz Parmesan cheese

2½ cups whole milk

3½ oz baby spinach

Preheat the oven to 350°F. Trim the fennel, peel the onions and potatoes, then roughly chop everything and put into a large pan on a medium heat with 1 tablespoon of oil. After 1 minute, pour in ¾ cup of water, pop the lid on and cook for 20 minutes, removing the lid halfway through.

Meanwhile, slice the bread into ¾-inch chunks. Drizzle over 1 tablespoon of oil and toss to coat, then scatter over a lined baking sheet and grate over the Parmesan. Bake for 25 minutes, or until beautifully golden and crisp.

Pour the milk into the pan. Bring to a boil, then ladle into a blender and whiz until super-smooth – you may need to work in batches. Season to perfection with sea salt and black pepper, then divide two-thirds of the soup between warm bowls. Add the spinach to the soup in the blender and whiz again. Randomly swirl or ripple the green soup between the bowls, and serve with the croutons.

> The green spinach swirl can be made with other delicate greens, such as watercress, arugula or tender Swiss chard, with fantastic results.

To make vegetarian: swap Parmesan for vegetarian hard cheese.

ENERGY	FAT	SAT FAT	PROTEIN	CARBS	SUGARS	SALT	FIBER
419kcal	15.1g	5.5g	15.6g	60.4g	14.6g	0.9g	10.3g

FRAGRANT NOODLE SOUP

ROASTED GINGER, LEMONGRASS, GARLIC & CHILI

SERVES 4 | 1 HOUR

5-inch piece of fresh ginger

2 stalks of lemongrass

1 bulb of garlic

4 long shallots

2 fresh red chilies

olive oil

8 cups vegetable stock

8 oz ripe cherry tomatoes,
    on the vine

6 kaffir lime leaves

1 oz dried porcini mushrooms

2 tablespoons red wine vinegar

2 tablespoons reduced-sodium
    soy sauce

7 oz mixed mushrooms

4½ oz baby corn

10 oz vermicelli rice noodles

1 lime

4 sprigs of fresh cilantro

Preheat the oven to 375°F. Crack and bash the unpeeled ginger, lemongrass and garlic bulb with the base of a large casserole pan, then place in the pan. Peel the shallots but keep them whole, then add to the pan with the chilies. Toss everything with 1 tablespoon of oil, then roast for 30 minutes.

Remove the pan from the oven, pour over the stock, then add the tomatoes (vines and all), kaffir lime leaves, porcini, vinegar and soy sauce. Simmer for 30 minutes over a medium-low heat on the stove, adding the mixed mushrooms and corn for the last 10 minutes. Cook the noodles according to the package instructions, then drain and divide between bowls. Squeeze the lime juice into the broth, then have a taste and tweak with a little more soy sauce, if needed. Spoon the soup over the noodles and finish with the cilantro leaves.

> Sometimes I buy and finely chop some kimchi and serve as a pickle on the side.

ENERGY	FAT	SAT FAT	PROTEIN	CARBS	SUGARS	SALT	FIBER
402kcal	6.2g	0.8g	15.8g	74.7g	5.1g	0.8g	5.6g

PULLED MUSHROOM SANDWICH

BLUE CHEESE NUGGETS, CRUMBLED WALNUTS & ARUGULA

SERVES 4 | 20 MINUTES

1 lb mixed mushrooms, such as oyster, shiitake, shimeji

extra virgin olive oil

herby or red wine vinegar

dried chili flakes

¼ of a red onion

2 stalks of celery, ideally with leaves

1 large ciabatta loaf

2 oz blue cheese

½ oz arugula

¾ oz shelled unsalted walnut halves

Preheat the oven to 350°F. Trim the mushrooms, then dry-fry in a large non-stick frying pan on a high heat for 5 minutes, turning regularly (this will bring out the nutty flavor) – you may need to work in batches. Meanwhile, drizzle 2 tablespoons each of oil and vinegar into a large bowl, and season with a good pinch of chili flakes, sea salt and black pepper. Peel the onion, finely chop with the celery and add to the bowl, adding the warm mushrooms as and when ready, and pulling any larger mushrooms apart into finer strands. Toss together.

Warm the ciabatta in the oven for 5 minutes, then slice in half and open it up like a book. Dot with nuggets of blue cheese, scatter over the arugula, crumble over the walnuts, then arrange the pulled mushroom mixture on top. Slice into 4 chunky portions and tuck in. I usually enjoy this with a seasonal salad.

> The filling for this sandwich can actually be served as a salad in its own right – tear the bread up into croutons for a tasty alternative.

ENERGY	FAT	SAT FAT	PROTEIN	CARBS	SUGARS	SALT	FIBER
289kcal	14.5g	4.1g	12g	29.4g	2.8g	1.2g	3.8g

MEDITERRANEAN VEGETABLE RICE
BOMBS OF GREEN PESTO, OLIVE TAPENADE, CREAMY MOZZARELLA & BASIL

SERVES 4 | 45 MINUTES

1½ cups basmati rice

1 small red onion

1 zucchini

4 ripe mixed-color tomatoes

¼ cup green pesto

olive oil

8 black olives (with pits)

white wine vinegar

extra virgin olive oil

4 sprigs of fresh basil

½ x 4½-oz ball of mozzarella cheese

Preheat the broiler to high. Tip the rice into a 14- x 10-inch roasting pan (or use a large round shallow ovenproof pan, like I've done here, if you have one), pour over 2⅔ cups of boiling salted water and cook over a medium heat for 12 minutes, stirring occasionally, then turn off the heat. Meanwhile, peel the red onion, then very finely slice with the zucchini, or use a mandolin (use the guard!). Finely slice the tomatoes into rounds.

Randomly bomb the pesto over the rice (if you fancy making pesto from scratch, take the recipe from page 90), then start layering up your veg: cover the rice with rounds of onion, then move on to a layer of zucchini, overlapping them as you go, followed by a layer of tomatoes. Repeat, moving slightly nearer the middle each time until you've covered the whole surface (use the picture to help you out – it might look a bit fiddly, but it's child's play to make). Drizzle with 2 tablespoons of olive oil and sprinkle with black pepper, then place under the broiler on the middle shelf for 25 minutes, or until beautifully gratinated. Meanwhile, for the tapenade, pit and very finely chop the olives, then mix with ½ a tablespoon each of vinegar and extra virgin olive oil. To serve, pick over the basil leaves, dot over the olive tapenade and delicately tear over the mozzarella.

> Very finely slicing the veg means you can pretty much use any kind or variety – baby carrots, fennel, eggplants, beets – to really celebrate the seasons in a flamboyant way.

To make vegetarian: use vegetarian pesto.

ENERGY	FAT	SAT FAT	PROTEIN	CARBS	SUGARS	SALT	FIBER
522kcal	26.4g	5.8g	11.9g	63.4g	5.7g	1.5g	3.2g

POTATO & MUSHROOM AL FORNO

GARLIC, CHIVES, TRUFFLED EGGS, COTTAGE CHEESE & PARMESAN

SERVES 4 | 1 HOUR 30 MINUTES

1½ lbs potatoes

2 onions

3 cloves of garlic

olive oil

7 oz button mushrooms

7 oz oyster mushrooms

3 large eggs

1 bunch of fresh chives (1 oz)

5 oz cottage cheese

½ teaspoon truffle oil

1 oz Parmesan cheese

Preheat the oven to 400°F. Scrub the potatoes and peel the onions, then cut into wedges. Place in a large roasting pan, bash and throw in the garlic cloves, then drizzle over 1 tablespoon of olive oil and season with sea salt and black pepper. Toss together well, then roast for 50 minutes, or until lightly golden and cooked through. Roughly slice the mushrooms, then toss in 1 tablespoon of olive oil and add to the pan for a final 20 minutes.

Meanwhile, beat the eggs until pale and fluffy, then finely chop and add the chives and fold through the cottage cheese and truffle oil (the tiniest amount makes all the difference – don't be tempted to add more). When the time's up, remove the pan from the oven, pour the egg mixture over the roasted veg and finely grate over the Parmesan. Bake for 10 minutes, or until beautifully golden and just set.

Delicious served with a lemony watercress salad.

> If you've got access to seasonal mixed wild mushrooms, this recipe is just crying out for them to be used, but is still delicious made with the humble, reliable farmed ones.

To make vegetarian: swap Parmesan for vegetarian hard cheese.

ENERGY	FAT	SAT FAT	PROTEIN	CARBS	SUGARS	SALT	FIBER
386kcal	15.8g	4.8g	18g	46.1g	8.9g	1.2g	6.4g

SCRUMPTIOUS VEG TRAYBAKE

SWEET TOMATO, CHIANTI, PORCINI, OLIVES, OREGANO & BAKED FETA

SERVES 4 | 1 HOUR 45 MINUTES

¾ oz dried porcini mushrooms

14 oz butternut squash

2 carrots

2 red onions

2 stalks of celery

2 red peppers

olive oil

2 cloves of garlic

10 black olives (with pits)

2 sprigs of fresh rosemary

½ teaspoon dried chili flakes

1 teaspoon dried oregano

1 cup Chianti red wine

2 x 14-oz cans of quality plum tomatoes

1 x 15-oz can of cannellini beans

4 oz feta cheese

1 oz arugula

1 lemon

Preheat the oven to 400°F. Cover the porcini with 6 tablespoons of boiling water. Scrub the squash (seed, if needed) and carrots, peel the onions, trim the celery and seed the peppers, then roughly chop and place in a large roasting pan with 1 tablespoon of oil. Peel and finely chop the garlic, pit and tear the olives, then add to the pan and strip in the rosemary leaves. Season with a pinch of sea salt and black pepper, the chili flakes and oregano, then toss together well and roast for 40 minutes, or until tender.

When the time's up, remove from the oven and pour over the wine. Scrunch in the tomatoes, tip in the beans (juices and all), and add the porcini and soaking liquor, leaving any gritty bits behind. Break over big chunks of feta and place back in the oven for 40 minutes, or until thickened and delicious. Dress the arugula with lemon juice and scatter over the pan before serving.

Delicious served with crusty sourdough bread or interesting grains, such as cracked wheat, freekeh, quinoa, couscous or wild rice – it also makes a fine pie filling.

ENERGY	FAT	SAT FAT	PROTEIN	CARBS	SUGARS	SALT	FIBER
374kcal	11.2g	4.8g	16.4g	41.7g	22.4g	2.3g	13.2g

FLORENTINA TRAYBAKE

ROOT VEG, CODDLED EGGS & LEMONY SPINACH SALAD

SERVES 4 | 1 HOUR 30 MINUTES

1 celery root

2 onions

1 lb Yukon Gold potatoes

3 mixed-color carrots

1 bunch of fresh chives (1 oz)

olive oil

1 tablespoon grainy mustard

4 large eggs

1 lemon

3½ oz baby spinach

extra virgin olive oil

Preheat the oven to 425°F. Peel and halve the celery root and onions, scrub the potatoes and carrots, then very finely slice (I like to cut the carrots into thin strips) and place in a large roasting pan. Finely chop and scatter over the chives, and season with a pinch of sea salt and black pepper. Drizzle with 2 tablespoons of olive oil, add the mustard, then toss together and shake into an even layer. Cover with aluminum foil and roast for 1 hour, then remove the foil and cook for a further 10 minutes, or until beautifully golden.

When the time's up, remove from the oven and make 4 little dents in the veg (right down to the bottom of the pan, if you can), crack in the eggs, season lightly with salt and pepper, then place back in the oven for 3 minutes, or until the eggs are cooked to your liking. Squeeze the lemon juice over the spinach, drizzle with 1 tablespoon of extra virgin olive oil, then toss to coat and serve alongside.

> In the summer, this is delicious made with new potatoes, baby carrots and beets.

ENERGY	FAT	SAT FAT	PROTEIN	CARBS	SUGARS	SALT	FIBER
345kcal	16.1g	3g	13.1g	39.7g	13.9g	1.4g	10.8g

PEA & RICOTTA STUFFED ZUCCHINI

CHERRY TOMATOES, OLIVES, MINT, LEMON & FLUFFY RICE

SERVES 4 | 45 MINUTES

4 sprigs of fresh mint

5 oz fresh or frozen peas

3½ oz ricotta cheese

1¾ oz sharp Cheddar cheese

1 lemon

8 baby zucchini, with flowers

14 oz ripe cherry tomatoes

4 scallions

8 black olives (with pits)

1 fresh red chili

2 cloves of garlic

olive oil

red wine vinegar

1½ cups basmati rice

Preheat the oven to 400°F. Pick the mint leaves into a food processor, then add the peas, ricotta and Cheddar. Finely grate in the lemon zest and squeeze in the juice, then add a pinch of black pepper and blitz until smooth. Taste and adjust the seasoning, if needed. Carefully fill each zucchini flower with the mixture, then press and pat the petals back together to seal.

Halve the tomatoes, trim and slice the scallions, and pit and tear the olives. Seed and roughly chop the chili, then peel and roughly chop the garlic. Put everything into a 14- x 10-inch roasting pan. Drizzle with 2 tablespoons each of oil and vinegar, then season with pepper and scrunch together well. Stir in the rice and 3 cups of boiling water, then place over the stove and bring to a boil, stirring occasionally. Lightly push the zucchini into the rice, and bake at the bottom of the oven for 20 minutes, or until beautifully golden.

Delicious with a summery salad and a glass of chilled dry white wine.

> If you can't get zucchini flowers, halve regular zucchini, then use a teaspoon to scrape out the seedy core and stuff them.

ENERGY	FAT	SAT FAT	PROTEIN	CARBS	SUGARS	SALT	FIBER
494kcal	16g	6g	18.4g	75g	5.6g	0.5g	5.5g

HASSELBACK AL FORNO

ROOT VEG GALORE, WILTED SPINACH, LENTILS & YOGURT RIPPLE

SERVES 4 | 1 HOUR 50 MINUTES

1 large parsnip

½ a butternut squash (1¼ lbs)

1 onion

2 beets

4 carrots

4 potatoes

2 cloves of garlic

½ a bunch of fresh thyme (½ oz)

olive oil

2 tablespoons white wine vinegar

6 tablespoons Chianti red wine

2 x 15-oz cans of green lentils

3½ oz baby spinach

¼ cup plain yogurt

Preheat the oven to 400°F. Scrub or peel all the veg: quarter the parsnip, squash and onion and halve the beets (try to choose medium-sized carrots and potatoes, but use your common sense and slice any larger ones in half). One at a time, place the veg on a board between the handles of two wooden spoons, so that when you slice down into them the spoons stop the blade from going all the way through. Carefully slice at just under ¼-inch intervals all the way along, putting the veg into a large roasting pan as you go.

Peel the garlic and place in a pestle and mortar, strip in the thyme leaves, then bash to a paste and muddle in 6 tablespoons of oil, the vinegar, and a pinch of sea salt and black pepper. Toss well with the veg, then roast for 1 hour, or until golden and caramelized, turning halfway. Remove all the veg to a board and place the pan over a medium heat on the stove. Pour in the wine and leave to bubble and cook away, scraping up all the sticky caramelized bits from the bottom of the pan. Tip in the lentils (juices and all) and spinach, then stir until the juices have thickened and the leaves have wilted. Season to taste with salt and pepper, ripple through the yogurt, then present to the table with the board of veg.

Delicious served with the rest of the bottle of red wine.

> Swapping out the lentils for borlotti, lima or cannellini beans, or even chickpeas, can be super-delicious — give it a try!

ENERGY	FAT	SAT FAT	PROTEIN	CARBS	SUGARS	SALT	FIBER
584kcal	22.6g	4g	16.8g	78g	23.1g	0.8g	18g

MASALA STUFFED PEPPERS

SPICY POTATO FILLING, PANEER CHEESE & SMASHED PISTACHIOS

SERVES 4 | 1 HOUR 35 MINUTES

1 lb potatoes

2 sweet potatoes (8 oz each)

1 red onion

4 cloves of garlic

1 fresh red chili

1 large knob of unsalted butter

1 teaspoon cumin seeds

¼ teaspoon ground cloves

2 teaspoons tomato paste

½ a bunch of fresh cilantro (½ oz)

2 red peppers

2 yellow peppers

red wine vinegar

2 oz paneer or feta cheese

¾ oz shelled unsalted pistachios

Scrub the potatoes and sweet potatoes and chop into ¾-inch chunks, then place in a large roasting pan over a medium heat on the stove. Cover with boiling salted water and cook for 15 minutes, or until tender, stirring occasionally, then drain.

Meanwhile, preheat the oven to 350°F. Peel and roughly chop the onion and garlic, and finely slice the chili. Place the pan back on the stove over a medium heat with the butter, add the onion, garlic, chili, cumin seeds, cloves, tomato paste and a good pinch of sea salt and black pepper, then cook for 3 minutes, stirring regularly. Finely chop most of the cilantro and add to the pan with the potatoes, then mix and mash everything together.

Carefully halve the peppers lengthways and seed, then rub the insides with a little vinegar and salt. Divide the filling between the peppers, then place back in the pan and roast for 1 hour, or until soft, sweet and beautifully gnarly, grating over the cheese for the last 5 minutes. Bash the pistachios in a pestle and mortar until fine. Serve half a red and yellow pepper on each plate, sprinkle with the pistachios and pick over the remaining cilantro leaves.

I love this served as it is, but it's also delicious as part of a bigger curry feast.

> I like to assemble this the day before and roast it when I need it. You can absolutely use this filling to stuff other veg, such as zucchini and eggplants.

ENERGY	FAT	SAT FAT	PROTEIN	CARBS	SUGARS	SALT	FIBER
389kcal	11.9g	5.5g	11.8g	62.5g	19.9g	1.2g	5.9g

RICE & NOODLES

ROASTED TOMATO RISOTTO

SWEET FENNEL, CRISPY THYME, GARLIC, VERMOUTH, PARMESAN

SERVES 6 | 1 HOUR

6 large ripe tomatoes

1 bulb of garlic

½ a bunch of fresh thyme (½ oz)

olive oil

5 cups vegetable stock

1 onion

1 bulb of fennel

2 knobs of unsalted butter

2 cups Arborio risotto rice

⅔ cup dry white vermouth

3 oz Parmesan cheese

Preheat the oven to 350°F. With a knife, cut the cores out of the tomatoes, then place cut-side down in a snug-fitting baking dish with the whole garlic bulb, and scatter over the thyme sprigs. Drizzle with 1 tablespoon of oil, season with sea salt, and roast for 1 hour, or until starting to burst open (the juices will add game-changing flavor later on).

Bring the stock to a simmer. Peel and finely chop the onion and fennel, reserving any herby tops, then place in a large, high-sided pan on a medium heat with 1 tablespoon of oil and 1 knob of butter. Cook for 10 minutes, or until softened but not colored, stirring occasionally, then stir in the rice to toast for 2 minutes. Pour in the vermouth and stir until absorbed. Add a ladleful of stock and wait until it's been fully absorbed before adding another, stirring constantly and adding ladlefuls of stock until the rice is cooked – it will need 16 to 18 minutes. Beat in the remaining knob of butter, finely grate and beat in the Parmesan, then season to perfection and turn the heat off. Cover the pan and leave to relax for 2 minutes so the risotto becomes creamy and oozy.

Divide the risotto between warm plates, place a tomato in the center with a little sweet garlic and the herby fennel tops, then drizzle over the tasty tomato juices.

> Squeezing the smooth, mild garlic out of its skin after roasting adds a delicious bonus flavor to the risotto.

To make vegetarian: swap Parmesan for vegetarian hard cheese.

ENERGY	FAT	SAT FAT	PROTEIN	CARBS	SUGARS	SALT	FIBER
507kcal	15.3g	6.9g	13.6g	77.7g	7.6g	0.7g	5.3g

SWEET & SOUR STIR-FRY

SWEET PEACHES, RAINBOW VEG, BOK CHOY & NOODLES

SERVES 4 | 20 MINUTES

1 tablespoon tomato paste

1 tablespoon cornstarch

1 tablespoon white wine vinegar

reduced-sodium soy sauce

1 teaspoon Chinese five-spice

1 x 14-oz can of peaches in
   natural juice

1 red onion

2 mixed-color peppers

1 carrot

4 cloves of garlic

1½-inch piece of fresh ginger

1 fresh red chili

olive oil

5 oz frozen peas

1 bok choy

7 oz vermicelli rice noodles

optional: 2 tablespoons
   sesame seeds

Mix the tomato paste and cornstarch together in a bowl, then muddle in the vinegar, 1 tablespoon of soy sauce and the five-spice. Drain and add the peach juices and mix well. Place a large non-stick frying pan or wok on a high heat. Peel the onion and seed the peppers, then finely slice with the carrot, adding them to the pan as you go. Dry-fry for 5 minutes, or until lightly charred, stirring occasionally. Peel the garlic and ginger, then finely chop with the chili and add to the pan with 1 tablespoon of oil. Fry for 2 minutes, then stir in the sauce. Roughly chop the peaches and add to the pan with the peas, then slice the bok choy into 8 and toss everything together. Season to taste with soy and black pepper.

Turn the heat down to low, then cook the noodles according to the package instructions and drain, reserving a cupful of starchy noodle water. Toast the sesame seeds in a dry frying pan until golden (if using). Adjust the consistency of the sauce with a splash of reserved noodle water, if needed, then serve with the noodles and a scattering of sesame seeds (if using).

I've opted for noodles here, but it's equally delicious with rice or steamed buns.

> I've used peaches in this story – I just love them – but apricots, and the more traditional pineapple, work well.

ENERGY	FAT	SAT FAT	PROTEIN	CARBS	SUGARS	SALT	FIBER
351kcal	6.9g	1.1g	8.1g	63.8g	16.6g	0.1g	7g

PUMPKIN RICE

CHERRY TOMATOES, LIMA BEANS & OKRA

SERVES 6 | 50 MINUTES

14 oz pumpkin or butternut squash

3½ oz coconut cream

4 allspice berries

4 scallions

½ a bunch of fresh thyme (½ oz)

2 Scotch bonnet chilies

½ a pointed cabbage (14 oz)

2¼ cups basmati rice

2 cloves of garlic

1 onion

olive oil

7 oz ripe mixed-color cherry tomatoes

7 oz okra

2 x 12-oz jars of lima beans

Peel and seed the pumpkin, then chop into ¾-inch chunks. Pour 3¼ cups of boiling salted water into a large pan over a medium-high heat, add the coconut cream and leave to melt, then add the pumpkin and allspice berries. Trim the scallions and bash with your fist, then halve and drop into the pan with half the thyme sprigs and the whole Scotch bonnets (no holes or bruises, please). Roughly chop the cabbage, discarding the core, then add to the pan with ½ a teaspoon each of sea salt and black pepper. Cover and cook for 10 minutes, then rinse and stir in the rice. Pop the lid back on, turn the heat down to low and cook for 12 minutes, or until the water is absorbed. Turn the heat off and leave to steam.

Meanwhile, peel and finely slice the garlic and peel and roughly chop the onion, then place in a large non-stick frying pan on a medium heat with 2 tablespoons of oil and cook for 5 minutes. Halve the tomatoes, then remove the chilies from the rice, carefully seed, slice, and add half to the pan (feel free to add more later, to taste, and remember to clean your knife, board and hands thoroughly after). Pick in the remaining thyme leaves, then trim and halve the okra and add to the pan. Cover and cook for 8 minutes, stirring occasionally, then tip in the beans (juices and all) to warm through for a few minutes. Fork up the rice, breaking up the pumpkin, and serve with the beans, seasoning everything to perfection.

> If you can't find pointed cabbage, feel free to use white or Savoy cabbage – or even Brussels and kale can be delicious.

ENERGY	FAT	SAT FAT	PROTEIN	CARBS	SUGARS	SALT	FIBER
513kcal	12.1g	6g	16.8g	89.9g	10.1g	0.4g	10g

MUSHROOM RISOTTO

CREAMY PARSLEY-SPIKED MASCARPONE

SERVES 6 | 1 HOUR

2 onions

2 cloves of garlic

3 stalks of celery

olive oil

2 knobs of unsalted butter

1 lb mixed mushrooms

1 lemon

extra virgin olive oil

5 cups vegetable stock

4 sprigs of fresh rosemary

2 cups Arborio risotto rice

¾ cup white wine

3 oz Parmesan cheese, plus extra
to serve

½ a bunch of fresh Italian parsley
(½ oz)

¼ cup mascarpone cheese

Peel and finely chop the onions, garlic and celery, then place in a large, high-sided pan over a medium heat with 1 tablespoon of olive oil and 1 knob of butter. Cook for 10 minutes, or until softened but not colored, stirring occasionally. Meanwhile, trim and slice any larger mushrooms, then dry-fry all the mushrooms in a large non-stick frying pan on a medium heat, until charred – you'll need to work in batches. Turn off the heat, then dress with the lemon juice, 2 tablespoons of extra virgin olive oil and a pinch of sea salt and black pepper. Remove and very finely chop half the mushrooms, keeping the rest warm until needed.

Bring the stock to a simmer, adding the rosemary to infuse. Stir the rice into the chopped veg to toast for 2 minutes. Pour in the wine and stir until absorbed. Add the chopped mushrooms and a ladleful of stock and wait until it's been fully absorbed before adding another, stirring constantly and adding ladlefuls of stock (avoiding the rosemary) until the rice is cooked – it will need 16 to 18 minutes. Beat in the remaining knob of butter, finely grate and beat in the Parmesan, then season to perfection and turn the heat off. Cover and leave to relax for 2 minutes so the risotto becomes creamy and oozy.

Meanwhile, pick the parsley leaves into a pestle and mortar and bash to a paste with a good pinch of salt. Muddle in the mascarpone, loosening with a splash of water, if needed. Divide the risotto between warm plates, dollop over the herby mascarpone, and top with the remaining mushrooms, drizzling over any juices. Finish with a fine grating of Parmesan.

To make vegetarian: swap Parmesan for vegetarian hard cheese.

ENERGY	FAT	SAT FAT	PROTEIN	CARBS	SUGARS	SALT	FIBER
577kcal	26g	13g	14.1g	71.5g	6.4g	1.1g	2.8g

VEGGIE PAD THAI

CRISPY FRIED EGGS, SPECIAL TAMARIND & TOFU SAUCE, PEANUT SPRINKLE

SERVES 2 | 30 MINUTES

5 oz rice noodles

sesame oil

¾ oz unsalted peanuts

2 cloves of garlic

3 oz silken tofu

reduced-sodium soy sauce

2 teaspoons tamarind paste

2 teaspoons sweet chili sauce

2 limes

1 shallot

11 oz crunchy veg, such as
    asparagus, broccolini,
    bok choy, baby corn

3 oz beansprouts

2 large eggs

olive oil

dried chili flakes

½ a romaine lettuce

½ a mixed bunch of fresh basil,
    mint and cilantro (½ oz)

Cook the noodles according to the package instructions, then drain and refresh under cold running water and toss with 1 teaspoon of sesame oil. Lightly toast the peanuts in a large non-stick frying pan on a medium heat until golden, then bash in a pestle and mortar until fine, and tip into a bowl. Peel the garlic and bash to a paste with the tofu, add 1 teaspoon of sesame oil, 1 tablespoon of soy, the tamarind paste and chili sauce, then squeeze and muddle in half the lime juice.

Peel and finely slice the shallot, then place in the frying pan over a high heat. Trim, prep and slice the crunchy veg, as necessary, then dry-fry for 4 minutes, or until lightly charred (to bring out a nutty, slightly smoky flavor). Add the noodles, sauce, beansprouts, and a good splash of water, toss together over the heat for 1 minute, then divide between serving bowls.

Wipe out the pan, crack in the eggs and cook to your liking in a little olive oil, sprinkling with a pinch of chili flakes. Trim the lettuce, click apart the leaves and place a few in each bowl. Pop the eggs on top, pick over the herbs, and sprinkle with the nuts. Serve with lime wedges for squeezing over, and extra soy, to taste.

If you want to make this dish vegan, remove the eggs and serve with extra cubes of tofu, marinated in soy and lime juice.

ENERGY	FAT	SAT FAT	PROTEIN	CARBS	SUGARS	SALT	FIBER
593kcal	19g	3.8g	26.4g	83.5g	10.7g	1.3g	8.3g

PRETTY PERSIAN-STYLE RICE

CRISPY SAFFRON CRUST, HERBS GALORE, POMEGRANATE & SMASHED PISTACHIOS

SERVES 6 | **50 MINUTES PLUS COOLING**

1 big pinch of saffron

2¼ cups basmati rice

3 cardamom pods

1 Yukon Gold potato

olive oil

1 red onion

1 big bunch of mixed fresh herbs,
such as dill, Italian parsley,
mint (2 oz)

¾ oz shelled unsalted pistachios

1 pomegranate

6 tablespoons plain yogurt

extra virgin olive oil

optional: rose harissa

Place the saffron in a bowl, cover with ⅓ cup of boiling water and leave to steep. Cook the rice in a large pan of boiling salted water for 7 minutes, cracking and adding the cardamom pods, then drain and spread out on a large baking sheet to cool. Season with a generous pinch of sea salt and black pepper, then divide into 4 piles, picking out and discarding the cardamom.

Scrub the potato and slice into ½-inch rounds. Rub a 10-inch non-stick frying pan with 1 tablespoon of olive oil, then add the potato in a single layer in a nice pattern and place on a medium-low heat. Toss the first pile of rice with half the saffron water, then add to the pan and carefully pat into an even layer. Add and pat down the second pile of rice, then peel, very finely slice and add a layer of onion. Top with the third pile of rice, then pick, finely chop and scatter over most of the herbs and cover with the remaining rice. Drizzle over the remaining saffron water, then find a plate just smaller than the pan, place on top and push down to really compact. Pop a lid on top, turn the heat down to low and cook for 20 minutes, or until golden and crisp. Meanwhile, roughly bash the pistachios in a pestle and mortar until fine. Halve the pomegranate, then, holding each half cut-side down, bash the back with a spoon so all the seeds come tumbling out.

Confidently turn the rice out onto a board, top with the yogurt, pomegranate seeds, remaining herbs, a drizzle of extra virgin olive oil and a scattering of pistachios. Absolutely delicious served with a dash of harissa, if you like.

> This layering of rice is so exciting. Feel free to mix up your herbs and even swap out pomegranate for grilled peaches, apricots or figs. So tasty!

ENERGY	FAT	SAT FAT	PROTEIN	CARBS	SUGARS	SALT	FIBER
338kcal	5.9g	1.3g	8.6g	66.6g	4.7g	0.7g	2.6g

MALAYSIAN-STYLE VEG NOODLES

BABY CORN, SNOW PEAS, TOFU, LIME & PEANUT SPRINKLE

SERVES 4 | 35 MINUTES

1 potato

2 shallots

olive oil

½ teaspoon ground turmeric

2 teaspoons curry powder

2 fresh kaffir lime leaves

2 cloves of garlic

¾-inch piece of fresh ginger

2 fresh red chilies

2 stalks of lemongrass

7 oz silken tofu

7 oz baby corn

1 x 14-oz can of light coconut milk

7 oz snow peas

reduced-sodium soy sauce

2 limes

¾ oz unsalted peanuts

7 oz rice noodles

Scrub the potato and peel the shallots, then chop into ½-inch dice and place in a large non-stick pan with 1 tablespoon of oil. Add the turmeric and curry powder, then cook on a medium-low heat for 20 minutes, or until lightly golden, stirring occasionally. Meanwhile, place the kaffir lime leaves in a pestle and mortar. Peel and roughly chop the garlic and ginger, trim and finely chop the chilies and lemongrass, then add them all to the lime leaves and bash to a fine paste. Scrape into the pan and cook for 5 minutes, stirring regularly. Roughly chop and add the tofu, followed by the corn, then pour in the coconut milk. Bring to a boil, stir in the snow peas, then season to taste with soy and lime juice.

Meanwhile, roughly chop the peanuts. Cook the noodles according to the package instructions, then drain and divide between 4 bowls. Spoon over the veg and sauce, sprinkle over the nuts, and serve with lime wedges for squeezing over.

> Sometimes I toss the chopped nuts through the noodles with a little lime zest before adding to the bowls – it makes them tacky, with a good crunch!

ENERGY	FAT	SAT FAT	PROTEIN	CARBS	SUGARS	SALT	FIBER
455kcal	15.5g	6.5g	13.7g	63.4g	6.8g	0.1g	2g

QUICK MUSHROOM NOODLE BROTH

QUICK CARROT & GINGER PICKLE, SCALLIONS & SESAME SEED SPRINKLE

SERVES 4 | 20 MINUTES

4 cloves of garlic

1½-inch piece of fresh ginger

peanut oil

1 oz dried porcini mushrooms

1 carrot

1 fresh red chili

1 teaspoon sushi pickled ginger

2 scallions

2 heaping tablespoons red
   miso paste

reduced-sodium soy sauce

7 oz dried egg noodles

2 bok choy

8 oz mixed mushrooms

1 tablespoon sesame seeds

Peel and finely slice the garlic and ginger, then place in a large casserole pan on a high heat with 1 tablespoon of oil. Fry for 2 minutes, add the porcini and 6 cups of boiling water, then cover and simmer on a low heat for 10 minutes. Meanwhile, scrub and coarsely grate the carrot with the chili, and mix with the sushi ginger. Trim and finely slice the scallions, then put both aside.

When the time's up, stir the miso paste and 2 tablespoons of soy sauce into the broth. Cook the noodles according to the package instructions, then divide between warm bowls. Season the broth to taste with soy and black pepper, then halve or quarter the bok choy and add with the mushrooms (they come in all shapes and sizes, so feel confident to tear, slice or leave whole) for just 1 minute, to keep their freshness. Divide the veg between the bowls, ladle over the steaming broth and serve with the pickle, scallions and a scattering of sesame seeds.

Delicious with a squeeze of lime juice, if you like.

> This broth welcomes any delicate veggies like snow peas, sugar snap peas, chard or baby corn, if you want to chop and change it to keep it interesting.

ENERGY	FAT	SAT FAT	PROTEIN	CARBS	SUGARS	SALT	FIBER
301kcal	7.4g	1.2g	13.4g	47.9g	4.2g	2.8g	3.5g

PASTA

GREENS MAC 'N' CHEESE

LEEK, BROCCOLINI & SPINACH, TOASTED ALMOND TOPPING

SERVES 6 | 1 HOUR

1 large leek

3 cloves of garlic

14 oz broccolini

3 tablespoons unsalted butter

½ a bunch of fresh thyme (½ oz)

2 tablespoons all-purpose flour

4 cups reduced-fat (2%) milk

16 oz dried macaroni

1 oz Parmesan cheese

5 oz sharp Cheddar cheese

3½ oz baby spinach

1¾ oz flaked almonds

Preheat the oven to 350°F. Trim, halve and wash the leek and peel the garlic, then finely slice with the broccolini stalks, reserving the florets for later. Place the sliced veg in a large casserole pan over a medium heat with the butter, then strip in the thyme leaves and cook for 15 minutes, or until softened, stirring regularly. Stir in the flour, followed slowly by the milk, then simmer for 10 minutes, or until thickened, stirring regularly. Meanwhile, cook the pasta in a large pan of boiling salted water for 5 minutes, then drain.

Grate the Parmesan and most of the Cheddar into the sauce, and mix well. Tip into a blender, add the spinach and whiz until smooth – you may need to work in batches. Season to perfection with sea salt and black pepper, then stir through the pasta and broccolini florets, loosening with a splash of milk, if needed. Transfer to a 14- x 10-inch baking dish, grate over the remaining Cheddar and scatter over the almonds. Bake for 30 minutes, or until beautifully golden and bubbling.

Swap spinach out for any kind of exciting fresh or frozen greens, discarding any tough stalks. I also sometimes add breadcrumbs to the top for bonus crunch. Tasty!

To make vegetarian: swap Parmesan for vegetarian hard cheese.

ENERGY	FAT	SAT FAT	PROTEIN	CARBS	SUGARS	SALT	FIBER
619kcal	25.1g	12.4g	29g	75.1g	12g	0.9g	6.4g

SWEET LEEK CARBONARA

FRESH THYME, GARLIC, CRACKED BLACK PEPPER & PARMESAN

2 large leeks

4 cloves of garlic

4 sprigs of fresh thyme

1 knob of unsalted butter

olive oil

10 oz dried spaghetti

1¾ oz Parmesan or pecorino cheese, plus extra to serve

1 large egg

Trim, wash and finely slice the leeks. Peel and finely slice the garlic and pick the thyme leaves, then place in a large casserole pan on a medium heat with the butter and 1 tablespoon of oil. Once sizzling, stir in the leeks and 1⅔ cups of water, then cover and simmer gently over a low heat for 40 minutes, or until sweet and soft, stirring occasionally. Season with sea salt and black pepper.

When the leeks are almost done, cook the pasta in a large pan of boiling salted water according to the package instructions, then drain, reserving a cupful of starchy cooking water. Toss the drained pasta into the leek pan, then remove from the heat and wait 2 minutes for the pan to cool slightly while you finely grate the cheese and beat it with the egg (if the pan's too hot, it'll scramble; get it right and it'll be smooth, silky and deliciously elegant).

Loosen the egg mixture with a splash of reserved cooking water, then pour over the pasta, tossing vigorously (the egg will cook in the residual heat). Season to absolute perfection, going a little OTT on the pepper. Adjust the consistency with extra cooking water, if needed, and finish with a little stroke of cheese.

Fantastic served with a glass of cold Italian white wine.

> Often I triple the leek base and freeze it for quick cooking another day.

To make vegetarian: swap Parmesan or pecorino for vegetarian hard cheese.

ENERGY	FAT	SAT FAT	PROTEIN	CARBS	SUGARS	SALT	FIBER
418kcal	14.4g	6g	17g	58.9g	4.4g	0.8g	2.3g

ODDS & ENDS PASTA ON TOAST

5-VEG TOMATO SAUCE, MELTED CHEESE, SMASHED BASIL

SERVES 4 | 55 MINUTES

olive oil

1 red onion

1 red pepper

1 zucchini

1 stalk of celery

4 cloves of garlic

2 x 14-oz cans of quality plum
tomatoes

1 tablespoon balsamic vinegar

5 oz mixed dried pasta

1 bunch of fresh basil (1 oz)

extra virgin olive oil

4 thick slices of granary-style
bread

2½ oz sharp Cheddar cheese

Place a large non-stick frying pan on a medium heat with 1 tablespoon of olive oil. Peel the onion and seed the pepper, then roughly chop with the zucchini and celery, adding them to the pan as you go. Peel, finely chop and add the garlic, then cook for 20 minutes, stirring regularly. Scrunch in the tomatoes, then add ½ a can's worth of water and the balsamic. Leave to tick away for 20 minutes, or until thickened and reduced, then season to taste with sea salt and black pepper.

Meanwhile, preheat the broiler to high. Cook the pasta in a large pan of boiling salted water according to the package instructions (stagger adding the pasta, if using different shapes and sizes), then drain and tip into the sauce. Pick most of the basil leaves into a pestle and mortar and bash to a fine paste with a pinch of salt, then muddle in 2 tablespoons of extra virgin olive oil.

Toast the bread on one side, then flip it over and grate over the Cheddar. Pop back under the broiler until bubbling, then spoon over the pasta and smashed basil, and finish with the remaining basil leaves. Seriously satisfying!

> I prefer to leave the sauce chunky, but if you've got fussy eaters (and that includes you, adults!), feel free to blend until smooth.

ENERGY	FAT	SAT FAT	PROTEIN	CARBS	SUGARS	SALT	FIBER
478kcal	18g	5.8g	18g	65g	16.2g	1.7g	8g

TASTY VEGAN LASAGNE

LAYERS OF PASTA, RICH TOMATO & CHIANTI RAGÙ, CREAMY MUSHROOM SAUCE

SERVES 6 | 3 HOURS

2 red onions

2 cloves of garlic

2 carrots

2 stalks of celery

2 sprigs of fresh rosemary

olive oil

1 teaspoon dried chili flakes

6 tablespoons vegan Chianti wine

1 x 15-oz can of green lentils

2 x 14-oz cans of quality plum tomatoes

2 lbs mixed wild mushrooms

4 heaping tablespoons all-purpose flour

3¼ cups almond milk

2½ oz vegan Cheddar cheese

10 oz dried lasagne sheets

½ a bunch of fresh sage (½ oz)

Peel the onions, garlic and carrots, trim the celery and pick the rosemary leaves, then finely chop. Scrape into a large pan on a medium heat with 2 tablespoons of oil and the chili flakes, and cook for 20 minutes, or until lightly golden. Pour in the wine and let it bubble and cook away, then tip in the lentils (juices and all). Scrunch in the tomatoes, add 1 can's worth of water, then simmer over a low heat for 1 hour. Season to perfection with sea salt and black pepper.

Meanwhile, working in batches, tear the mushrooms into a large non-stick frying pan on a medium heat and dry-fry for 5 minutes (this will bring out the nutty flavor), then transfer to a plate. Quickly wipe the pan, then pour in ¼ cup of oil and stir in the flour. Gradually whisk in the almond milk, simmer for 5 minutes to thicken, then pour into a blender. Add a third of the mushrooms and 1¾ oz of the cheese, season with salt and pepper, then blitz until smooth. Preheat the oven to 350°F.

Spoon a layer of tomato sauce into the bottom of a 14- x 10-inch baking dish, scatter over a few mushrooms, then cover with lasagne sheets and 5 tablespoons of creamy sauce. Repeat these layers three more times, finishing with all the remaining creamy sauce and mushrooms. Grate over the remaining cheese. Pick the sage, toss in a little oil, then push into the top layer. Bake at the bottom of the oven for 50 minutes, or until golden and bubbling. Leave to stand for 15 minutes before serving. Delicious served with a simple seasonal salad.

A handful of baby spinach scattered between the layers is always a nice addition.

Make sure you use vegan lasagne sheets.

ENERGY	FAT	SAT FAT	PROTEIN	CARBS	SUGARS	SALT	FIBER
539kcal	20.2g	4.8g	15.4g	75g	12.8g	1g	8g

SPAGHETTI PORCINI BALLS

SWEET & SPICY SUN-DRIED TOMATO, BASIL & PARMESAN SAUCE

SERVES 6 | 40 MINUTES

¾ oz dried porcini mushrooms

2 x 8-oz packages of ready-made mixed grains, ideally with punchy flavor

2 large eggs

3½ oz baby spinach

2 fresh red chilies

1 lemon

1¾–2½ oz stale breadcrumbs

olive oil

16 oz dried spaghetti

1 clove of garlic

1 bunch of fresh basil (1 oz)

¾ oz Parmesan cheese, plus extra to serve

3½ oz sun-dried tomatoes in oil

Cover the porcini with boiling water, leave for 5 minutes, then drain, reserving the soaking water. Place the grains in a food processor with the porcini mushrooms, eggs, spinach and one of the chilies. Finely grate in the lemon zest, then add a pinch of sea salt and black pepper and whiz until sticky. Pulse in the breadcrumbs, adding just enough to bring the mixture together – packages of grains will vary, so use your common sense. With wet hands, roll into 30 little balls. Drizzle 1 tablespoon of oil into a large non-stick frying pan over a medium heat, then add the balls and fry for 10 minutes, or until golden all over, turning with care – you may need to work in batches (keep warm covered with aluminum foil, if necessary).

Cook the pasta in a large pan of boiling salted water according to the package instructions, then drain, reserving a cupful of starchy cooking water. Meanwhile, give the food processor a quick rinse, then peel and drop in the garlic, pick in most of the basil leaves, finely grate in the Parmesan, and add the sun-dried tomatoes with 2 tablespoons of oil from the jar. Add the remaining chili (seed, if you like), then whiz to a paste. Pulse in the reserved porcini soaking water, then toss with the drained pasta, adding a splash of reserved cooking water to loosen, if needed. Fold through the porcini balls, and finish with the reserved basil leaves, a generous squeeze of lemon juice and a fine grating of Parmesan.

Serve with a lemony green salad for added crunch and zing. It's a winner!

> I find I get better results from the grain packages that have been jazzed up a little bit, rather than the plain naked ones.

To make vegetarian: swap Parmesan for vegetarian hard cheese.

ENERGY	FAT	SAT FAT	PROTEIN	CARBS	SUGARS	SALT	FIBER
628kcal	19.4g	3.8g	23g	92.2g	6.1g	1.6g	8.4g

PICNIC PASTA SALAD

NEON DRESSING, CHERRY TOMATOES, MOZZARELLA & OLIVES

SERVES 4 | 15 MINUTES

10 oz dried pasta shells

¼ of a clove of garlic

1 bunch of fresh Italian
    parsley (1 oz)

1 bunch of fresh basil (1 oz)

red wine vinegar

extra virgin olive oil

½ a celery heart

8 oz ripe mixed-color
    cherry tomatoes

12 black olives (with pits)

4½-oz ball of mozzarella cheese

Cook the pasta in a large pan of boiling salted water according to the package instructions, then drain. Meanwhile, peel the garlic and put into a blender with the herbs, 2 tablespoons each of vinegar and oil, and a good splash of water, then whiz until smooth. Season to perfection with sea salt and black pepper.

Very finely chop the celery heart and quarter the tomatoes, then place in a large salad bowl. Pit and tear in the olives, pour over the vivid green dressing and tip in the drained pasta, then toss together. Serve hot, warm or cold, tearing over the mozzarella just before serving.

Amazing served as part of a buffet or picnic, and great packed up for lunch.

> If you have any leftovers, crack in an egg or two, toss together, then grate over some cheese and bake until beautifully golden.

ENERGY	FAT	SAT FAT	PROTEIN	CARBS	SUGARS	SALT	FIBER
436kcal	16.2g	6g	16.8g	59.2g	4.2g	0.7g	3.7g

SUNSHINE FUSILLI PASTA

SWEET YELLOW PEPPER SAUCE, CRUSHED PISTACHIOS & PARMESAN

SERVES 4 | 20 MINUTES

1 onion

2 cloves of garlic

olive oil

2 tablespoons white wine
vinegar

2 yellow peppers

¾ oz shelled unsalted pistachios

10 oz dried fusilli

1 oz Parmesan cheese, plus
extra to serve

Peel and finely slice the onion and garlic, then place in a large non-stick frying pan on a medium heat with 1 tablespoon of oil, the vinegar and a pinch of sea salt. Seed and finely slice the peppers, then add to the pan and cook with the lid on for 10 minutes, or until softened but not colored, stirring occasionally. Meanwhile, bash the pistachios in a pestle and mortar until fine.

Cook the pasta in a large pan of boiling salted water according to the package instructions, then drain, reserving a cupful of starchy cooking water. Finely grate the Parmesan into a blender, add the pepper mixture and a splash of boiling water, then whiz until smooth and season with salt and black pepper. Toss the pasta and sauce together, loosening with a splash of reserved cooking water, if needed. Finish with a dusting of pistachios and a fine grating of Parmesan.

Always good with a fresh crunchy herby green salad.

> As obvious as it sounds, this dish can be made to great effect using red, orange or green peppers, all giving a slightly different expression of color and flavor.

To make vegetarian: swap Parmesan for vegetarian hard cheese.

ENERGY	FAT	SAT FAT	PROTEIN	CARBS	SUGARS	SALT	FIBER
388kcal	9.6g	2.4g	13.8g	65.4g	8.8g	0.7g	2.6g

SILKY ZUCCHINI BOW-TIES

CHILI, GARLIC, FENNEL, CREAM & PARMESAN

SERVES 4 | 15 MINUTES

10 oz dried farfalle

4 cloves of garlic

1 fresh red chili

olive oil

½ teaspoon fennel seeds

2 mixed-color zucchini

6 tablespoons rosé wine

⅓ cup heavy cream

1½ oz Parmesan cheese,
   plus extra to serve

Cook the pasta in a large pan of boiling salted water according to the package instructions, then drain, reserving a cupful of starchy cooking water. Meanwhile, peel the garlic and finely chop with the chili, then place in a large non-stick frying pan on a medium heat with 1 tablespoon of oil and the fennel seeds. Coarsely grate the zucchini (discard the seedy core), then add to the pan and cook for 5 minutes, or until softened, stirring occasionally.

Turn the heat up to high, pour in the wine, leave to bubble and cook away, then switch off and add the cream. Grate over the Parmesan, tip in the pasta and toss together, loosening with a splash of reserved cooking water, if needed. Season to taste with sea salt and black pepper and finish with a fine grating of Parmesan.

If you want to up your summertime veg, a delicious side salad of lemony dressed baby spinach and fresh raw peas makes a really good match.

> Vary the grated veg used in this dish – butternut squash, carrots, fennel, even peppers – for tasty results.

To make vegetarian: swap Parmesan for vegetarian hard cheese.

ENERGY	FAT	SAT FAT	PROTEIN	CARBS	SUGARS	SALT	FIBER
404kcal	11.7g	5.1g	14.9g	59.7g	4.2g	0.3g	0.9g

SUMMER TAGLIATELLE

BASIL & ALMOND PESTO, BROKEN POTATOES, DELICATE GREEN VEG

SERVES 4 | 20 MINUTES

1 bunch of fresh basil (1 oz)

½ a clove of garlic

1¾ oz blanched almonds

extra virgin olive oil

¾ oz Parmesan cheese, plus
extra to serve

¼ of a lemon

1 Yukon Gold potato

4½ oz green beans

10 oz dried tagliatelle

7 oz delicate summer veg, such as
fava beans, peas, broccolini

Pick most of the basil leaves into a pestle and mortar and bash to a paste with a pinch of sea salt. Peel and bash in the garlic, then pound in the almonds until fine. Muddle in ¼ cup of oil, finely grate in the Parmesan, then squeeze in the lemon juice. Season to perfection, and tweak to your liking.

Scrub and finely slice the potato, trim just the stalks off the beans, then place both in a pan of boiling salted water with the tagliatelle and cook according to the pasta package instructions. Prep the delicate summer veg as necessary, adding them to the pan for the last 3 minutes. Drain, reserving a cupful of starchy cooking water, then toss with the pesto, loosening with a splash of reserved cooking water, if needed. Drizzle with 1 tablespoon of oil, and finish with the remaining basil and a fine grating of Parmesan. Nice served with a crunchy seasonal salad.

> I've used fresh basil and almonds here, but pretty much any soft herb and unsalted shelled nut combo will deliver very tasty results – whatever you fancy!

To make vegetarian: swap Parmesan for vegetarian hard cheese.

ENERGY	FAT	SAT FAT	PROTEIN	CARBS	SUGARS	SALT	FIBER
561kcal	25.9g	4.1g	18.4g	67.9g	5g	0.6g	5.7g

MIGHTY MUSHROOM PASTA

SWEET TOMATO & PARMESAN SAUCE, GARLICKY HAZELNUT BREADCRUMBS

SERVES 4 | 20 MINUTES

1¾ oz stale breadcrumbs

olive oil

¾ oz blanched hazelnuts

4 cloves of garlic

3 sprigs of fresh thyme

14 oz mixed mushrooms

1 teaspoon dried chili flakes

1 x 14-oz can of quality plum tomatoes

10 oz dried penne

1 oz Parmesan cheese, plus extra to serve

Tip the breadcrumbs into a medium non-stick frying pan on a low heat with 1 tablespoon of oil. Lightly crush the hazelnuts in a pestle and mortar, add to the pan, then peel and finely grate in 2 cloves of garlic and strip in the thyme leaves. Toss regularly throughout the pasta and sauce process, until golden and crisp.

Place a large non-stick frying pan on a high heat, then tear or roughly slice the mushrooms (depending on their size and shape) and dry-fry for 1 minute (this will bring out their nutty flavor). Peel, finely chop and add the remaining garlic, with the chili flakes and 1 tablespoon of oil, then cook for 3 minutes, tossing regularly. Scrunch in the tomatoes, add 1 can's worth of water and leave to tick away. Meanwhile, cook the pasta in a large pan of boiling salted water according to the package instructions, then drain, reserving a cupful of starchy cooking water.

Finely grate the Parmesan, then toss with the pasta and sauce, loosening with a splash of reserved cooking water, if needed. Season to taste, and top with the toasty hot sprinkle and a fine grating of Parmesan.

> You can easily add a creamy dimension to the sauce by adding 1 tablespoon of crème fraîche or cream, which is super-delicious and indulgent.

To make vegetarian: swap Parmesan for vegetarian hard cheese.

ENERGY	FAT	SAT FAT	PROTEIN	CARBS	SUGARS	SALT	FIBER
465kcal	15.5g	3.4g	17.5g	68.1g	6.3g	0.4g	5.6g

SQUASH GNOCCHI

FRAGRANT PARSLEY & WALNUT PESTO

SERVES 4 | 1 HOUR 15 MINUTES

1 lb Yukon Gold potatoes

1 lb butternut squash

⅔ cup Tipo 00 flour, plus extra
for dusting

1 whole nutmeg, for grating

1 bunch of fresh Italian parsley
(1 oz)

½ a clove of garlic

1¾ oz shelled unsalted walnut
halves

extra virgin olive oil

1 oz Parmesan cheese, plus
extra to serve

½ a lemon

Peel the potatoes and squash (seed, if needed), chop into 1¼-inch chunks and cook in a large pan of boiling salted water for 12 minutes, or until tender, then drain and cool. Tip onto a clean kitchen towel, gather up into a bundle and squeeze out as much liquid as you can, then tip into a bowl. Mash together, then sprinkle over the flour, finely grate over half the nutmeg, season generously with sea salt and black pepper, and mix well. Knead the mixture on a flour-dusted surface for a few minutes until pliable, then divide into 4 equal pieces and roll each into a sausage, about ¾ inch thick. Slice into ¾-inch pieces to create the gnocchi.

Pick the parsley leaves into a pestle and mortar and bash to a paste with a pinch of salt. Peel and bash in the garlic, then pound in the walnuts until fine. Muddle in ¼ cup of oil, finely grate in the Parmesan, then squeeze in the lemon juice. Season to perfection and tweak to your liking.

When you're ready to eat, cook the gnocchi in two batches in a pan of boiling salted water for 2 to 3 minutes – as soon as they come up to the surface they're ready, so remove with a slotted spoon to a plate – they'll firm up after about 30 seconds. Either toss each batch with half the pesto and a splash of cooking water, or spread the pesto on a plate and serve the steaming gnocchi on top. Finish with an extra grating of Parmesan. Delicious with a seasonal salad.

I love having fun with the pesto, so swap the parsley for arugula or a blend of mint and basil. Store-bought jars are great if you're short on time, but making your own will give you super-fresh, incomparable flavor.

To make vegetarian: swap Parmesan for vegetarian hard cheese.

ENERGY	FAT	SAT FAT	PROTEIN	CARBS	SUGARS	SALT	FIBER
447kcal	23.4g	4g	11.8g	49.7g	7.5g	1.1g	4.4g

SALADS

ROAST NEW POTATO & PICKLE SALAD

ZINGY LEMON, MUSTARD, LOADSA HERBS & CRUMBLED FETA

SERVES 6 | 1 HOUR

2½ lbs new potatoes

olive oil

6 cloves of garlic

1 lemon

2 sprigs of fresh rosemary

1 tablespoon all-purpose flour

1 English cucumber

3½ oz radishes, ideally with leaves

½ a red onion

1 teaspoon grainy mustard

2 tablespoons red wine vinegar

½ a bunch of fresh dill (½ oz)

½ a bunch of fresh mint (½ oz)

1½ oz feta cheese

Preheat the oven to 400°F. Cook the potatoes in a large pan of boiling salted water for 20 minutes, then drain and steam dry. Tip into a large roasting pan and drizzle with 2 tablespoons of oil, then add a good pinch of sea salt and black pepper. Bash and add the unpeeled garlic cloves to the pan, then roast for 20 minutes. Meanwhile, finely grate the lemon zest and pick and finely chop the rosemary. When the time's up, scatter the lemon zest, rosemary and flour over the potatoes from a height. Toss together, then squash flat with a potato masher and roast for a final 20 minutes, or until golden and crisp.

Meanwhile, scratch the outside of the cucumber with a fork to create grooves, then finely slice into rounds. Halve and quarter the radishes, peel and very finely slice the onion, then put all this into a bowl with the mustard, vinegar and half the lemon juice. Season to taste with salt and pepper, pick and add the herb leaves, toss together, then place on top of the hot crispy potatoes, mixing just before serving. Finish with a crumbling of feta, and extra lemon juice, if you like.

> I have had some fun making this salad with hasselback potatoes for added texture and crunch – see page 106 for the technique.

ENERGY	FAT	SAT FAT	PROTEIN	CARBS	SUGARS	SALT	FIBER
223kcal	6.5g	1.7g	6.4g	34.7g	4.3g	0.7g	4.7g

LADY MARMALADE SALAD

ENDIVE, SWEET SHALLOTS, ORANGE DRESSING & CRUSHED NUTS

SERVES 4 | 25 MINUTES

2 tablespoons mixed shelled unsalted nuts, such as walnut halves, almonds, pistachios

2 large shallots

4 oranges

1 tablespoon red wine vinegar

extra virgin olive oil

1 heaping teaspoon liquid honey

4 mixed-color endive

½ a bunch of fresh chervil (½ oz)

Toast the nuts in a large dry frying pan over a medium heat until golden, then bash in a pestle and mortar until fine. Peel the shallots and slice ¼ inch thick, then dry-fry for 5 minutes, or until lightly charred, tossing regularly. Juice the oranges, pour into the pan and simmer until syrupy, then remove from the heat. Add the vinegar, 3 tablespoons of oil and the honey, then season to perfection with sea salt and black pepper (it should be slightly too acidic and salty, to make the magic happen).

Halve the endive, finely slice the base end, then click the leaves apart and place in a salad bowl. Spoon over the warm dressing, pick over the chervil leaves and sprinkle with the crushed nuts, then toss to dress.

Brilliant with goat's cheese and hot toasts, plus a glass of dry white wine.

> Works well with any kind of bitter salad leaves.

ENERGY	FAT	SAT FAT	PROTEIN	CARBS	SUGARS	SALT	FIBER
156kcal	12.5g	1.7g	2.1g	11.1g	8.7g	0.5g	0.6g

DOUBLE CORN SALAD

CRUNCHY ICEBERG LETTUCE & CREAMY CHEESE DRESSING

SERVES 4–6 | 30 MINUTES

canola oil

¼ cup popping corn

chipotle Tabasco sauce

4 corn on the cob

1 iceberg lettuce

4 scallions

1 oz sharp Cheddar cheese

1 oz blue cheese

6 tablespoons plain yogurt

¼ of a clove of garlic

2 teaspoons English mustard

2 tablespoons white wine vinegar

1 teaspoon Worcestershire sauce

4 sprigs of fresh cilantro

Place a large non-stick frying pan on a high heat with 1 tablespoon of oil, then add the popping corn and cover with a lid. Once popped, add a few generous shakes of Tabasco, toss together and tip into a large salad bowl. In the same pan, sear the corn until lightly charred all over, turning regularly, then remove.

Trim and roughly chop the lettuce, and trim and finely slice the scallions, then add to the bowl. Break the cheeses into a blender, and spoon in the yogurt. Peel and add the garlic, followed by the mustard, vinegar and Worcestershire sauce, then blitz until smooth, and season to taste with sea salt and black pepper. Carefully slice off the corn kernels and add to the bowl. Pour over the dressing, toss together and pick over the cilantro leaves, then serve straight away.

Really nice as a tasty lunch served with warm wraps or as part of a bigger spread.

Some other things this salad loves for company are sliced avocado, crumbled feta and halved green grapes – it's a really fun dish!

To make vegetarian: use anchovy-free Worcestershire sauce.

ENERGY	FAT	SAT FAT	PROTEIN	CARBS	SUGARS	SALT	FIBER
248kcal	12.5g	4.5g	11.9g	22.5g	6.8g	0.7g	2.1g

MY CHOPPED FATTOUSH SALAD

GRILLED PITA, RAINBOW CHOPPED SALAD & POMEGRANATE GALORE

SERVES 4 | 20 MINUTES

4 pita breads

1 pomegranate

1 tablespoon sumac

extra virgin olive oil

1 lemon

1 tablespoon pomegranate
   molasses

2 mixed-color peppers

1 bulb of fennel

½ an English cucumber

2 ripe tomatoes

2 scallions

1 romaine lettuce

1 big bunch of mixed fresh
   herbs, such as mint, dill,
   Italian parsley (2 oz)

Toast the pitas on a grill pan on a high heat until crisp and bar-marked, then roughly chop and put aside. Halve the pomegranate and, holding each half cut-side down in your fingers, bash the back of it with a spoon so all the seeds tumble out into a large salad bowl. Sprinkle over the sumac, then drizzle in 2 tablespoons of oil, squeeze over the lemon juice and add the pomegranate molasses.

Seed the peppers and finely chop with the fennel, cucumber (discard the watery core) and tomatoes, trim and finely slice the scallions and lettuce, and add to the bowl. Pick and finely chop the herb leaves, scatter into the bowl with the pita and toss together. Season to taste with sea salt and black pepper.

Amazing with little raw peas when in season, and if you can't get pomegranate, little cubes of chopped mango are also delicious in the mix.

ENERGY	FAT	SAT FAT	PROTEIN	CARBS	SUGARS	SALT	FIBER
287kcal	8g	1.2g	9.2g	46.4g	13.5g	0.8g	6g

SHAVED FENNEL, MELON & MOZZARELLA

CRISPY CAPERS, MINT & CHILI, STICKY BALSAMIC DRESSING

SERVES 4 | 15 MINUTES

olive oil

2 tablespoons baby capers

4 sprigs of fresh mint

1 fresh red chili

¼ cup balsamic vinegar

1 super-ripe cantaloupe melon

2 bulbs of fennel

1 small red onion

8 bocconcini mozzarella (5 oz)

Drizzle 2 tablespoons of oil into a large non-stick frying pan. Scatter in the capers, pick in the mint leaves, then finely slice and add the chili. Fry gently on a medium heat for 5 minutes, or until crispy, jiggling the pan regularly. Turn the heat off, remove everything to a little dish with a slotted spoon, then pour the balsamic into the scented warm oil and let it sizzle. Scoop the melon seeds into a sieve and press them to squeeze all the sweet juice into the hot pan, then discard the seeds. Use a teaspoon to remove little nuggets and curls of melon to a bowl.

Trim the fennel, reserving any herby tops, and peel the red onion, then very finely slice both by hand or on a mandolin (use the guard!). Place in icy water for 2 minutes to crisp up, then drain well and pat dry with a clean kitchen towel (this will stop the dressing from getting watered down). Toss with the melon, and season to perfection with sea salt and black pepper. Serve the salad on a platter or individual plates, scatter over the mozzarella, crispy mint, capers and chili, and the reserved herby fennel top, and drizzle over the dressing.

Don't think about making this unless you have a lovely ripe melon that's sweet and perfumed.

ENERGY	FAT	SAT FAT	PROTEIN	CARBS	SUGARS	SALT	FIBER
241kcal	14.7g	6.1g	10.1g	17.5g	16.2g	0.7g	7g

FRENCH GARLIC BREAD SALAD

DELICATE LEAVES, GRAPES, HERBS & THICK MUSTARDY DRESSING

SERVES 6 | 45 MINUTES PLUS PROVING

1 x ¼-oz package of dried yeast

3⅓ cups bread flour, plus extra
    for dusting

4 cloves of garlic

1 bunch of fresh Italian parsley
    (1 oz)

11 tablespoons unsalted butter
    (at room temperature)

extra virgin olive oil

2 tablespoons Dijon mustard

2 tablespoons white wine vinegar

1 teaspoon liquid honey

½ a bunch of fresh chives (½ oz)

7 oz mixed-color grapes

2 oz shelled unsalted walnut
    halves

10 oz delicate salad leaves, such
    as frisée, arugula, radicchio

Whisk the yeast into 1⅓ cups of lukewarm water, leave for 2 minutes, then pour into a large bowl with the flour and a good pinch of sea salt. Mix up as best you can, then knead vigorously on a flour-dusted surface to give you a smooth, elastic dough. Place in the bowl, cover with a clean damp kitchen towel and proof for 1 hour in a warm place, or until doubled in size. Knock out the air with your fists, then divide into 6, shape into ovals about ½ inch thick, and proof on a flour-dusted baking sheet for 30 minutes. Preheat the oven to 425°F.

Meanwhile, make the flavored butter. Peel the garlic and pick the parsley leaves, then finely chop and scrunch into the butter with a pinch of salt and black pepper. Lightly press small pieces of flavored butter into the bread, then bake for 15 minutes, or until golden and cooked through.

Whisk 6 tablespoons of oil with the mustard, vinegar, honey and a pinch of salt and pepper in a large bowl to make an emulsified dressing. Finely chop the chives, slice the grapes and walnuts, then toss with the salad leaves and dressing and place on top of the hot bread (strangely, I always get a lot of satisfaction out of serving fridge-cold salad with oven-hot bread – seriously good!).

I sometimes like to serve this with shaved or crumbled goat's cheese. Yum!

> I find that the best-tasting grapes always have seeds – sometimes you've just got to halve and seed them for the most delicious experience.

ENERGY	FAT	SAT FAT	PROTEIN	CARBS	SUGARS	SALT	FIBER
703kcal	41.1g	15.9g	13.5g	74.7g	7.9g	1.1g	4.1g

ANGRY BEAN SALAD

WARM ARRABBIATA DRESSING, CHILLED BABY MOZZARELLA, FRESH MINT

SERVES 4 | 20 MINUTES

14 oz ripe mixed-color cherry tomatoes

14 oz green and yellow beans

4 sprigs of fresh mint

4 cloves of garlic

2 fresh red chilies

olive oil

3 tablespoons red wine or balsamic vinegar

8 bocconcini mozzarella (5 oz)

4 slices of rustic bread

Carefully plunge the tomatoes into a pan of fast-boiling salted water for exactly 30 seconds, scoop out with a sieve and run under cold water. Line up the beans, remove just the stalk ends and place in the boiling water for 4 minutes. Meanwhile, pick the mint leaves, putting the baby leaves aside for garnish. Peel the garlic, then finely slice with the chilies. Pinch and peel away the tomato skins, reserving the flesh (it's a bit of a faff, but it's worth it).

Drain the beans, placing the pan back on a medium heat. Drizzle in 1 tablespoon of oil, then add the garlic, chilies and mint leaves. Fry for 2 minutes, add the tomatoes, vinegar and beans and simmer for 4 minutes, stirring regularly to break up the tomatoes. Taste and season to absolute perfection with sea salt and black pepper, then spoon onto a platter along with any tasty juices.

Scatter over the mozzarella and reserved mint leaves, and serve with hot toast.

Lovely served warm on the day – and any leftovers are great cold in a lunch box.

ENERGY	FAT	SAT FAT	PROTEIN	CARBS	SUGARS	SALT	FIBER
296kcal	11.9g	5.8g	13.8g	33.4g	7.2g	1g	5.6g

VIBRANT BHEL PURI SALAD

PUFFED RICE, POMEGRANATE, PAPPADAMS & PEANUTS

SERVES 4 | 20 MINUTES

¾-inch piece of fresh ginger

2 teaspoons tamarind chutney

extra virgin olive oil

1 pomegranate

1 lemon

1¾ oz unsalted peanuts

3½ oz puffed rice

1 red onion

1 English cucumber

7 oz ripe mixed-color
cherry tomatoes

10 radishes, ideally with leaves

1 fresh green chili

½ a bunch of fresh mint (½ oz)

½ a bunch of fresh cilantro
(½ oz)

2 uncooked pappadams

½ teaspoon garam masala

1¾ oz Bombay mix

Peel and roughly chop the ginger and bash to a paste in a pestle and mortar, then add the tamarind chutney and 1 tablespoon of oil. Squeeze in the juice from half the pomegranate and all of the lemon, then muddle together and tip into a large salad bowl. Toast the peanuts and puffed rice in a large dry non-stick frying pan on a medium heat until lightly golden (keep an eye on them, as they can easily catch), then remove from the heat and tip into the bowl.

Peel and very finely chop the onion, finely chop the cucumber, quarter the tomatoes and halve the radishes, then add to the bowl. Slice and add the chili (seed, if you like), and pick in the herb leaves. Holding the remaining pomegranate half cut-side down, bash the back of it with a spoon so all the seeds come tumbling out into the bowl. Puff up the pappadams in the microwave for 30 seconds each, then scrunch over the bowl, and sprinkle over the garam masala and Bombay mix. Toss everything together well, and serve straight away.

Really nice with a dollop of cilantro yogurt.

> This makes an exciting portable salad – put the dressing into the bottom of a container and layer the rest of the salad ingredients on top, then simply shake up just before eating.

ENERGY	FAT	SAT FAT	PROTEIN	CARBS	SUGARS	SALT	FIBER
329kcal	15g	2.4g	10.8g	37.7g	10.3g	0.8g	5.5g

SQUASHED CAULI & CHERRY SALAD

HERBY NUTTY BROWN RICE, PRESERVED LEMON & TOASTED PINE NUTS

SERVES 4 | 50 MINUTES

1 large head of cauliflower,
    ideally with leaves (2 lbs)

1½ cups brown rice

olive oil

2 teaspoons za'atar

7 oz ripe cherries

1 preserved lemon

1 lemon

1 teaspoon liquid honey

extra virgin olive oil

2 tablespoons pine nuts

1 bunch of fresh mint (1 oz)

1 bunch of fresh dill (1 oz)

¼ cup plain Greek yogurt

Preheat the oven to 425°F. Remove just the tatty outer leaves from the cauliflower, then break into large florets. Cook the rice in a large pan of boiling salted water according to the package instructions, adding the florets and leaves for just the first 10 minutes to parboil, then remove them to a large roasting pan with a slotted spoon. Drizzle the cauliflower with 2 tablespoons of olive oil, season with a pinch of sea salt, black pepper and the za'atar, and toss to coat. Place another pan on top, push down to really squash and flatten, then place in the oven (still with the pan on top) for 30 minutes, or until golden and crisp.

Meanwhile, pit and roughly chop the cherries, finely chop the preserved lemon, discarding any pips, and place in a bowl. Squeeze in half the lemon juice, drizzle with the honey and 3 tablespoons of extra virgin olive oil, and mix well.

Drain the rice and leave to steam dry. Toast the pine nuts in a dry non-stick frying pan on a medium heat until golden. Squeeze the remaining lemon juice over the rice and season to taste with salt and pepper. Pick and finely chop the herbs, toss with the rice and tip onto a platter. Top with the cauliflower, yogurt, pine nuts and the lemony cherry mixture (juices and all).

> Feel free to swap in your favorite soft herbs, depending on what you've got at home. Plus, any kind of unsalted nuts or seeds work well in this story.

ENERGY	FAT	SAT FAT	PROTEIN	CARBS	SUGARS	SALT	FIBER
568kcal	25.1g	4.8g	15.8g	74.1g	16.3g	0.9g	7.8g

EASY THAI-STYLE NOODLE SALAD

CRUNCHY VEG, LOADSA HERBS, SUPER-FRESH DRESSING, NUTS & SEEDS

SERVES 4 | 20 MINUTES

7 oz vermicelli rice noodles

2-inch piece of fresh ginger

3 limes

1 tablespoon reduced-sodium
   soy sauce

1 tablespoon chili jam

extra virgin olive oil

sesame oil

4 scallions

1½ lbs mixed crunchy veg, such
   as carrots, bok choy, Napa
   cabbage, radishes, endive,
   asparagus, sprouts

3 oz unsalted peanuts

1 tablespoon sesame seeds

½ a bunch of fresh mint (½ oz)

½ a bunch of fresh cilantro
   (½ oz)

Cook the noodles according to the package instructions, then drain and refresh under cold running water. Meanwhile, peel and roughly chop the ginger, then bash to a paste in a pestle and mortar. Finely grate in the lime zest and squeeze in the juice, then add the soy sauce, chili jam, 2 tablespoons of extra virgin olive oil and 1 teaspoon of sesame oil. Muddle together and tip into a large salad bowl.

Take pride in slicing the veg really nicely: trim and very finely slice the scallions and whatever other crunchy veg you choose, and add to the dressing. Toast the peanuts and sesame seeds in a dry non-stick frying pan on a medium heat until golden, then bash half to a powder in a pestle and mortar and tip into the bowl, saving the rest for garnish. Add the noodles to the bowl, then pick and tear in the herb leaves and toss together well, scattering over the reserved nuts and seeds. Season with black pepper and extra soy, if you like.

Sometimes I like to serve this dish with soy-doused silken tofu – delicious!

> I often make this salad to use up odds and ends in the fridge, which means it's always a little bit different – a great recipe for minimizing food waste.

ENERGY	FAT	SAT FAT	PROTEIN	CARBS	SUGARS	SALT	FIBER
437kcal	18.2g	3.1g	11.5g	55.5g	10.6g	0.5g	3.6g

WARM GRAPE & RADICCHIO SALAD

TOASTED PINE NUTS, GARLIC, ROSEMARY, STICKY BALSAMIC & HONEY

SERVES 4 | 30 MINUTES

7 oz seedless red grapes

1 radicchio or 2 red endive

2 cloves of garlic

2 sprigs of fresh rosemary

2 heaping tablespoons pine nuts

olive oil

2 tablespoons balsamic vinegar

1 tablespoon liquid honey

1 oz arugula

Put the grapes on a grill pan over a high heat and grill for 5 minutes, or until caramelized and starting to burst open, then place in a large salad bowl. Trim and quarter the radicchio, then dismantle all the leaves. Working in batches, grill, char and soften on both sides, then add to the bowl (this may feel like a very unusual process, but trust me, it's delicious).

Once you've grilled the radicchio, turn the heat off (we're going to use the pan to make a warm dressing). Peel and finely slice the garlic, pick the rosemary leaves and place in the still-hot grill pan with the pine nuts and 2 tablespoons of oil. Keep everything moving for 1 minute, then add the balsamic vinegar (it'll sizzle and smell amazing!) and pour every last bit into the bowl along with the honey. Toss and massage it all together, seasoning to absolute perfection with sea salt and black pepper. Leave to sit for 10 minutes, then toss through the arugula.

Great as a side salad, or shave over a little goat's cheese and serve with hot toast.

This salad makes a surprisingly amazing pizza topping with bombs of mozzarella. Enjoy!

ENERGY	FAT	SAT FAT	PROTEIN	CARBS	SUGARS	SALT	FIBER
209kcal	13.6g	1.5g	2.9g	20.1g	17.8g	0.1g	2.6g

BURGERS & FRITTERS

INDIAN-STYLE CHIP BUTTY

SPICED POTATO, MANGO & POMEGRANATE CHUTNEY, MINT YOGURT & SPRINKLES

SERVES 4 | 35 MINUTES

14 oz potatoes

14 oz sweet potatoes

3 cloves of garlic

1¼-inch piece of fresh ginger

1 fresh red chili

1 large knob of unsalted butter

1 teaspoon garam masala

1 teaspoon mustard seeds

2 tablespoons mango chutney

½ a pomegranate

1 bunch of fresh mint (1 oz)

¼ cup plain yogurt

4 soft rolls

¾ oz Bombay mix

Scrub the potatoes and sweet potatoes and chop into ¾-inch chunks, cook in a large pan of boiling salted water for 10 minutes, or until tender, then drain and steam dry. Peel the garlic and ginger, finely chop with the chili, and place in a large non-stick frying pan over a medium heat with the butter, garam masala and mustard seeds. After 1 minute, tip and mash in the potatoes, then season to perfection with sea salt and black pepper. Keep frying until crispy, then mix up and allow to get crispy again. Divide roughly into 4 (still in the pan), then use 2 spoons to crudely mold and shape into balls, patiently frying and turning until kind of rounded, really golden and crispy all over (trust me, these are amazing!).

Spoon the mango chutney into a bowl, squeeze in enough pomegranate juice to loosen, then mix together with a handful of the pomegranate seeds. Whiz the mint leaves in a blender with the yogurt until smooth. Split the rolls open and lightly toast on the inside, and roughly crush the Bombay mix.

Spoon a dollop of mint yogurt onto each bun base, top with a hot potato ball, a little mango chutney and Bombay mix, then pop the lid on and squash.

> As another option, these are also great torn into a chapati with a mixed chopped salad and a squeeze of lemon juice for an Indian-style wrap.

ENERGY	FAT	SAT FAT	PROTEIN	CARBS	SUGARS	SALT	FIBER
470kcal	11.4g	5.2g	12.8g	84.6g	14g	1.3g	3.6g

CORN & JALAPEÑO FRITTERS

CARAMELIZED BANANA, AVOCADO, TOMATO & FETA SALAD

SERVES 4 | 35 MINUTES

1 cup self-rising flour

1 cup reduced-fat (2%) milk

1 cup frozen corn

1 large egg

1 heaping tablespoon pickled
    jalapeño chilies

2 oz feta cheese

1 English cucumber

4 ripe mixed-color tomatoes

2 tablespoons red wine vinegar

½ a bunch of fresh cilantro
    (½ oz)

2 scallions

1 ripe avocado

4 ripe bananas

olive oil

Put the flour, milk and corn into a bowl, crack in the egg, and season with a pinch of black pepper. Finely chop and add the jalapeño chilies, then crumble in half the feta and whisk to a thick batter.

Roughly chop the cucumber and tomatoes, then place in a salad bowl with the vinegar. Pick and roughly chop most of the cilantro leaves, trim and finely slice the scallions, then add to the bowl with a pinch of pepper and toss together. Quarter, pit and peel the avocado.

For the best results, cook one portion at a time: peel one of the bananas and halve lengthways, then place cut-side down to one side of a large non-stick frying pan over a medium heat with 1 teaspoon of oil. Spoon 2 separate ladlefuls of batter into the pan, and cook until the fritters are golden on both sides and the banana is caramelized. Repeat with the remaining ingredients, dividing the salad, avocado, remaining feta and cilantro between the plates as you go.

> Frozen and canned corn is amazing, but for the ultimate experience, remove the kernels from fresh corn cobs.

ENERGY	FAT	SAT FAT	PROTEIN	CARBS	SUGARS	SALT	FIBER
562kcal	18.1g	5.4g	18.2g	82.2g	26.2g	3.1g	5.1g

ROASTED BLACK BEAN BURGERS

ZINGY SALSA, YOGURT, SLICED MANGO & AVOCADO

SERVES 4 | **40 MINUTES**

1½ red onions

7 oz mixed mushrooms

3½ oz rye bread

ground coriander

1 x 15-oz can of black beans

olive oil

1½ oz sharp Cheddar cheese

4 soft rolls

3½ oz ripe cherry tomatoes

1 lime

chipotle Tabasco sauce

1 ripe mango

1 ripe avocado

¼ cup plain yogurt

4 sprigs of fresh cilantro

Preheat the oven to 400°F. Peel 1 onion, place in a food processor with the mushrooms, rye bread and 1 teaspoon of ground coriander, and whiz until fine. Drain and pulse in the black beans, season lightly with sea salt and black pepper, then divide into 4 and shape into patties, roughly 1 inch thick. Rub all over with oil and dust with ground coriander, then place on an oiled baking sheet and roast for 25 minutes, or until dark and crispy, topping with the Cheddar and warming the rolls for the last few minutes.

Meanwhile, peel and very finely chop the remaining onion with the tomatoes and place in a bowl. Squeeze over the lime juice, add a few shakes of Tabasco and season to taste. Pit, peel and finely slice the mango and avocado.

Halve the warm rolls and divide the yogurt between the bases, followed by half the salsa, the mango, avocado and cilantro leaves. Top with the burgers, remaining salsa and extra Tabasco, pop the lids on and press down lightly.

Always nice with oven-roasted, skin-on chips.

> Make sure you choose the ripest possible tomatoes for the salsa – the flavor is incomparable!

ENERGY	FAT	SAT FAT	PROTEIN	CARBS	SUGARS	SALT	FIBER
499kcal	18.7g	5.3g	19g	64g	14.1g	1.6g	12.5g

SPICED CARROT PANCAKES

SILKY HUMMUS, CRUNCHY VEG, ROSE HARISSA & CRUSHED PISTACHIOS

SERVES 4 | 20 MINUTES

5 oz carrots

1 fresh green chili

½ a bunch of fresh cilantro (½ oz)

½ a red onion

1 teaspoon ground cumin

½ teaspoon fennel seeds

1 cup whole-wheat
   self-rising flour

1 cup reduced-fat (2%) milk

1 large egg

olive oil

3½ oz crunchy veg, such as
   radishes, carrots, cucumber

2 teaspoons rose harissa

1 lemon

¼ cup go-to hummus
   (see page 242)

1 oz watercress

optional: 1½ oz feta cheese

1 oz shelled unsalted pistachios

Scrub the carrots and coarsely grate into a large bowl. Finely chop and add the chili and cilantro, peel, finely slice and add the onion, then scatter over the spices. Add the flour, milk, egg, and mix well.

Place a large non-stick frying pan on a medium-low heat and drizzle in 1 teaspoon of oil. Working in batches, spoon in 2 tablespoons of batter per pancake (the rougher the better – the sprawly bits will give you great texture and crunch). Cook until golden on both sides, pressing lightly after you turn, then repeat.

Meanwhile, finely slice the crunchy veg, and mix harissa with half the lemon juice. Serve 2 pancakes at a time hot from the pan, topped with a dollop of go-to hummus (see page 242), a pinch of crunchy veg and some watercress. Crumble over the feta (if using) and drizzle over the lemony harissa. Bash the pistachios in a pestle and mortar until fine, then scatter on top and serve with lemon wedges for squeezing over.

> Once you've mastered this recipe, why not give it a try with grated beets, squash or zucchini? Super-delicious!

ENERGY	FAT	SAT FAT	PROTEIN	CARBS	SUGARS	SALT	FIBER
411kcal	15.3g	3.9g	17.9g	54.4g	8.7g	1g	9g

BRILLIANT BHAJI BURGER

CILANTRO YOGURT, MANGO CHUTNEY, CRUNCHY PAPPADAM SPRINKLE

SERVES 4 | 40 MINUTES

1 red onion

2 cloves of garlic

2 fresh green chilies

1 big bunch of fresh
 cilantro (2 oz)

2½ oz paneer cheese

7 oz butternut squash

1½-inch piece of fresh ginger

⅔ cup all-purpose flour

1 lime

2 teaspoons rogan josh
 curry paste

olive oil

⅓ cup plain yogurt

1 little gem lettuce

4 soft burger buns

2 uncooked pappadams

mango chutney

Peel and very finely slice the onion and garlic, seed and finely slice the chilies, finely chop the cilantro stalks, reserving the leaves, then place in a bowl. Coarsely grate in the paneer and squash (seed, if needed), then peel and finely grate in the ginger. Sprinkle in the flour and a pinch of sea salt and black pepper, then squeeze over the lime juice. Add the curry paste and 3 tablespoons of water, then mix.

Drizzle 2 tablespoons of oil into a large non-stick frying pan over a medium-low heat, then roughly divide the mixture into 4 portions and place in the pan, flattening them out into rough rounds, about the width of the buns (don't worry about wispy edges, it'll mean bonus crunch later!). Fry for 16 minutes, or until golden and cooked through, turning every few minutes. Meanwhile, pound most of the cilantro leaves to a paste in a pestle and mortar, muddle in the yogurt, then season to taste. Finely shred the lettuce, halve the burger buns (warm first, if you like), and puff up the dry pappadams in the microwave for 30 seconds each.

Divide the cilantro yogurt between the bases and inside bun lids, then break up the pappadams and sprinkle over. Place a crispy bhaji burger on top of each bun base, add a dollop of mango chutney, a few cilantro leaves and the lettuce, then pop the tops on and press down lightly.

Serve with a cold beer and extra fresh chili if you love a bit of heat (like me!).

> You can have a lot of fun with this recipe by mixing up not only the veg you choose but also the curry paste.

ENERGY	FAT	SAT FAT	PROTEIN	CARBS	SUGARS	SALT	FIBER
493kcal	15.4g	4.8g	17g	75.2g	20.7g	1.9g	6.2g

ROGAN JOSH SCOTCH EGGS

RUNNY GOLDEN YOLKS, CRISPY NAAN BREADCRUMBS & MANGO CHUTNEY

SERVES 4–8 | **50 MINUTES PLUS CHILLING**

5 large eggs

2 x 8-oz packages of ready-made mixed grains, ideally with punchy flavor

2 heaping teaspoons rogan josh curry paste

1 bunch of fresh mint (1 oz)

⅓ cup all-purpose flour

1 naan bread

8 cups vegetable oil, for frying

mango chutney

Soft-boil 4 eggs in a pan of boiling salted water on a medium-high heat for 5 minutes exactly, then drain, cool under cold running water, and peel. Tip the grains into a food processor with the curry paste, pick in the mint leaves, then whiz until fairly fine and tacky in texture, adding a splash of water, if needed. Divide into 4 balls. One at a time, pat out on a 6-inch square of parchment paper, to just under ½ inch thick. Place the paper flat on your hand, put a peeled egg in the center and mold the mixture up and around the egg to seal it inside, using the paper to help you. As it comes together into a ball, remove it from the paper and press gently in your hands to create the perfect covering – patch up any holes as you go. Place the flour in one bowl, beat the remaining egg in another, then whiz the naan to fine crumbs and tip into a third bowl. Cover the coated eggs with flour, dip into the beaten egg and roll in the crumbs until well covered, then chill.

When you're ready to cook, just under half-fill a large sturdy pan with oil – the oil should be 3 inches deep, but never fill your pan more than half full – and place on a medium-high heat. Use a thermometer to tell when it's ready (325°F), or add a piece of potato and wait until it turns golden – that's the sign that it's ready to go. Carefully lower the Scotch eggs into the pan using a slotted spoon and cook for 8 minutes, or until golden. Scoop out and drain on paper towel. Cut in half and serve seasoned lightly with sea salt and with mango chutney for dunking.

Fantastic with salad for dinner, or serve up half as a starter or lighter bite.

Super-fun made with double yolker eggs if you can get your hands on some!

ENERGY	FAT	SAT FAT	PROTEIN	CARBS	SUGARS	SALT	FIBER
674kcal	43.3g	6.6g	21.7g	48.7g	1.8g	1.7g	5.7g

ROASTED FALAFEL PITA POCKETS

SILKY TAHINI, CHOPPED SALAD, CRISPY CHICKPEAS & GARLIC, POMEGRANATE

SERVES 4 | I HOUR

2 x 15-oz cans of chickpeas

olive oil

2 cloves of garlic

½ teaspoon each dried chili
    flakes, fennel seeds, cumin
    seeds, ground coriander

1 big bunch of mixed fresh herbs,
    such as Italian parsley, cilantro,
    mint (2 oz)

7 oz frozen peas

4 ripe tomatoes

½ an English cucumber

extra virgin olive oil

1 lemon

½ a pomegranate

4 large pita breads

¼ cup tahini

Preheat the oven to 400°F. Drain the chickpeas, placing a handful into a small non-stick ovenproof frying pan over a medium heat with 3 tablespoons of olive oil. Peel, finely slice and add the garlic, then cook until golden, stirring regularly while you whiz up the falafel mix. Working quickly, place the spices in a food processor with a pinch of sea salt and black pepper. Tear in the herbs, discarding the stalks, then tip in the remaining chickpeas and the peas and whiz to combine, keeping a bit of texture. Remove the chickpeas and garlic to paper towel with a slotted spoon, leaving the flavored oil behind. Carefully add the falafel mix to the hot flavored oil and press out with a spatula to flatten and fill the pan. Fry for 5 minutes, then roast for 40 minutes, or until golden and crisp.

Meanwhile, finely chop the tomatoes and cucumber and scrape into a bowl. Drizzle lightly with extra virgin olive oil, squeeze over the lemon juice and season with salt and pepper. Holding the pomegranate half cut-side down in your fingers, bash the back of it with a spoon so all the seeds tumble into another bowl.

Warm the pitas in the oven for 2 minutes, then cut strips off one side and open up to create pita pockets. Loosen the tahini with a splash of water, if needed, then rub 1 tablespoon around the inside of each pita pocket. Randomly stuff with a quarter of the falafel, breaking and pushing it in, then load up with as much salad and pomegranate as you can fit in. Finish with the crispy chickpeas and garlic, and serve any leftover salad on the side.

> Jazz this up even more by serving with a dollop of harissa-swirled yogurt — seriously good!

ENERGY	FAT	SAT FAT	PROTEIN	CARBS	SUGARS	SALT	FIBER
540kcal	24.8g	3.6g	20.6g	61.9g	9.7g	1.6g	11.7g

ONE-PAN WONDERS

SCRUFFY EGGPLANT LASAGNE

SWEET TOMATO SAUCE WITH GARLIC, SAGE & LEMON, CHEESE & ALMOND CRUNCH

SERVES 6 | I HOUR 35 MINUTES

3 large eggplants (14 oz each)

3 onions

6 cloves of garlic

1 bunch of fresh sage (1 oz)

olive oil

1 teaspoon dried chili flakes

1 lemon

2 x 14-oz cans of quality
   plum tomatoes

3 oz sharp Cheddar cheese

3 oz Parmesan cheese

10 oz fresh lasagne sheets

1¾ oz blanched almonds

Place a large shallow casserole pan on a medium heat with 1 cup of water. Halve the eggplants lengthways and place in the pan. Peel, quarter and add the onions, then cover with a lid and cook for 20 minutes. Meanwhile, peel and finely slice the garlic, and pick the sage leaves. Preheat the oven to 400°F.

Remove the lid, and once most of the liquid has cooked away, make a well in the middle. Add 3 tablespoons of oil, the garlic, chili flakes and most of the sage leaves, then finely grate in the lemon zest. Once golden, scrunch in the tomatoes, pour in 2 cans' worth of water, and simmer for 20 minutes, stirring occasionally.

Remove the pan from the heat, grate in the cheeses, then season to absolute perfection with sea salt and black pepper. Tear in the pasta sheets and mix up really well to coat and separate, then pull some of the sheets to the top to create a top layer. Bash the almonds until fine and rub the remaining sage leaves with oil, then sprinkle on top. Use the back of a spoon to create some dips and wells, and bake for 25 minutes, or until golden and bubbling.

I love this served with a big crunchy green salad dressed with balsamic vinegar.

> Two of my girls are gluten-intolerant, so I often turn this into a pasta bake by using gluten-free pasta. Feel free to use any pasta shape. Simply parboil before adding.

To make vegetarian: swap Parmesan for vegetarian hard cheese.

ENERGY	FAT	SAT FAT	PROTEIN	CARBS	SUGARS	SALT	FIBER
463kcal	22.9g	7.5g	20.1g	48.4g	16.3g	0.6g	5.7g

SUMMER BUBBLE & SQUEAK

CHILI FRIED EGGS, APPLE & WATERCRESS SALAD, FRENCH DRESSING

SERVES 4 | 1 HOUR

1¼ lbs baby new potatoes

5 oz fresh or frozen peas

5 oz fresh or frozen fava beans

¼ of a Savoy cabbage (8 oz)

1 zucchini

1 carrot

olive oil

4 large eggs

1 fresh red chili

extra virgin olive oil

1 teaspoon Dijon mustard

1 tablespoon red wine vinegar

1 eating apple

1½ oz watercress

Scrub the potatoes and cook in a large pan of boiling salted water for 20 minutes, or until tender, adding the peas and fava beans for the last minute, then drain. Meanwhile, trim the cabbage and zucchini and scrub the carrot, then roughly chop into ½-inch chunks. Place them all in a 10-inch non-stick frying pan on a medium heat with 1 tablespoon of olive oil and cook for 15 minutes, or until golden and caramelized, then add the potatoes, peas and fava beans. At this point, start to mash it all up – keep mashing and frying for 15 minutes. Season to taste with sea salt and black pepper, pat down and flatten for a final 5 minutes, or until golden and crisp, then turn out onto a platter.

Fry the eggs to your liking in the same pan, finely slicing and scattering the chili over the egg. Pour 2 tablespoons of extra virgin olive oil into a large bowl, and whisk in the mustard and vinegar. Matchstick the apple, toss in the dressing with the watercress, and serve alongside the bubble and squeak and eggs.

> If this is what summer looks like, imagine how gorgeous winter could also be – think chestnuts, squash, Brussels sprouts, mushrooms. Wow!

ENERGY	FAT	SAT FAT	PROTEIN	CARBS	SUGARS	SALT	FIBER
373kcal	17.4g	3.4g	16.8g	40.4g	12.7g	0.4g	9.6g

PROPER BAKED BEANS

SWEET TOMATO & PEPPER SAUCE, CHEDDAR, ROSEMARY & CRISPY STODGY BREAD

SERVES 6 | 1 HOUR 10 MINUTES

1 red onion

2 cloves of garlic

1 carrot

1 fresh red chili

olive oil

1 teaspoon sweet smoked
    paprika

1 tablespoon cider vinegar

1 x 16-oz jar of roasted peppers
    in brine

1 x 14-oz can of quality plum
    tomatoes

1 level teaspoon black treacle
    or dark brown sugar

4 x 15-oz cans of beans, such as
    butter, cannellini

½ a loaf of rustic bread (8 oz)

2 oz sharp Cheddar cheese

4 sprigs of fresh rosemary

Preheat the oven to 400°F. Peel the onion and garlic, and scrub the carrot, then whiz in a food processor with the chili until finely chopped. Tip into a large non-stick ovenproof frying pan over a medium heat with 1 tablespoon of oil and the paprika, then fry for 15 minutes, or until lightly caramelized, stirring regularly. Add the vinegar and leave to cook away, then tip back into the food processor with the peppers (juices and all) and tomatoes and whiz until smooth. Pour back into the pan, add the treacle and bring to a boil. Tip in the beans (juices and all), then simmer for 5 minutes, while you slice the bread ½ inch thick.

Coarsely grate the cheese and stir through the beans, then season to perfection with sea salt and black pepper. Fan the bread over the top of the pan, patching up any gaps, then lightly push it down into the sauce and rub a little sauce over the top. Pick the rosemary leaves and toss with a little oil, then sprinkle over the top. Bake for 30 minutes, or until golden and gnarly (you're aiming for the perfect contrast between crisp and wonderfully stodgy).

Nice served as the main event or as a side – I like it with a crispy tangy salad.

> This is a great opportunity to try different beans, or even chickpeas.

ENERGY	FAT	SAT FAT	PROTEIN	CARBS	SUGARS	SALT	FIBER
384kcal	9.2g	3.3g	20.3g	56.5g	11g	0.6g	12.3g

GREEK-INSPIRED CAULIFLOWER STEW

OLIVES, ZINGY LEMON, FRESH TOMATOES, NEW POTATOES & PEAS

SERVES 4 | 1 HOUR 25 MINUTES

1 lemon

olive oil

1 bulb of garlic

2 red onions

10 black olives (with pits)

10 oz new potatoes

½ a bunch of fresh oregano
 (½ oz)

10 large ripe plum tomatoes

1 head of cauliflower, ideally with
 leaves (1¾ lbs)

7 oz fresh or frozen peas or
 fava beans

Preheat the oven to 400°F. Use a vegetable peeler to strip the lemon zest into a large casserole pan on a medium heat, then add 2 tablespoons of oil and the garlic bulb. Peel and quarter the onions and separate into petals, pit the olives, and slice the potatoes ½ inch thick. Add to the pan, pick in the oregano leaves and cook for 5 minutes, or until just starting to soften and color. Quarter and add the tomatoes, then season to taste with sea salt and black pepper.

Pour 2 cups of water into the pan and bring to a boil, stirring well and scraping up any sticky bits from the bottom. Discard just the tatty outer leaves from the cauliflower, then cut a cross into the stalk and push it right down to the bottom of the pan. Drizzle with 1 tablespoon of oil, cover, then place in the oven for 1 hour, or until golden and caramelized, basting occasionally and removing the lid halfway through. Remove the cauliflower to a serving platter and pick out the garlic bulb, then place the pan back over a medium heat on the stove, stir in the peas or fava beans, and simmer for 5 minutes. Carefully squeeze all the garlic out of the skins and stir back into the pan. Taste and tweak the seasoning, if needed, then pour over the cauliflower and finish with a good squeeze of lemon juice.

I love to serve this with bread to mop up the juices – heavenly!

When adding the peas or fava beans, this is your opportunity to add extra quick-cooking greens like chard, spinach, asparagus, broccolini – this will lift the dish and really reflect the seasons.

ENERGY	FAT	SAT FAT	PROTEIN	CARBS	SUGARS	SALT	FIBER
311kcal	12.3g	1.9g	11.9g	41g	21.2g	0.3g	11.9g

TOMATO & SPRING VEG FRITTATA

PEAS, ASPARAGUS, RICOTTA & FRESH MINT

SERVES 4 | 2 HOURS 15 MINUTES

6 large ripe tomatoes

1 teaspoon dried oregano

8 large eggs

1¾ oz Parmesan cheese

2 oz fresh peas

10 oz asparagus

½ a bunch of fresh mint (½ oz)

olive oil

4½ oz ricotta cheese

Preheat the oven to 275°F. Halve and seed the tomatoes, then place in a 10-inch non-stick ovenproof frying pan and season with sea salt and black pepper. Sprinkle over the oregano, roast for 1 hour 30 minutes, then remove.

Turn the temperature up to 400°F. Crack the eggs into a large bowl and whisk until pale and fluffy. Grate in most of the Parmesan, add the peas and season with a pinch of salt and pepper. Use a vegetable peeler to peel the asparagus into ribbons, discarding the woody ends, then pick and finely chop the mint leaves, adding both to the bowl and mixing together.

As soon as the oven is up to temperature, remove the tomatoes from the pan and drizzle in 1 tablespoon of oil. Pour in the egg mixture, then place the tomatoes back on top. Spoon over little nuggets of ricotta, and grate over the remaining Parmesan. Bake for 18 minutes, or until golden and just set.

Nice served with a hunk of crusty bread.

> I love making these dehydrated tomatoes, but if you haven't got time, swap in sun-dried tomatoes – it's no trouble at all!

To make vegetarian: swap Parmesan for vegetarian hard cheese.

ENERGY	FAT	SAT FAT	PROTEIN	CARBS	SUGARS	SALT	FIBER
340kcal	23.7g	8.5g	25.6g	8g	6.4g	1.7g	3.5g

ANGRY PASTA FAGIOLI

SQUASH, BEANS, WARMING CHILI, ROSEMARY OIL

SERVES 4 | 50 MINUTES

10 oz butternut squash

1 carrot

olive oil

4 fresh red chilies

1 onion

2 cloves of garlic

10 oz dried whole-wheat penne

1 x 15-oz can of borlotti beans

1 x 14-oz can of quality plum tomatoes

2 sprigs of fresh rosemary

extra virgin olive oil

1 teaspoon red wine vinegar

Peel the squash (seed, if needed) and scrub the carrot, then chop into ½-inch chunks and place in a large casserole pan on a medium heat with 2 tablespoons of olive oil. Prick and throw in the whole chilies (this will give you a warming, gentle heat), then cook for 10 minutes, or until lightly golden, stirring regularly. Peel and finely chop the onion and garlic, then add to the pan and cook for a further 10 minutes, or until softened and caramelized.

Wrap the pasta in a clean kitchen towel and give it a good bash with a rolling pin to crack and break it up, then stir into the pan with a pinch of sea salt and black pepper. Tip in the beans (juices and all) and scrunch in the tomatoes, along with 3 cans' worth of water. Pop the lid on and simmer for 20 minutes, or until thickened and the pasta is cooked, stirring occasionally.

Meanwhile, strip the rosemary leaves into a pestle and mortar, add a pinch of salt and bash to a paste, then muddle in 3 tablespoons of extra virgin olive oil and the vinegar. Swirl into the pan and serve up.

> I like to pull out the chilies, chop them into a paste and serve them as an angry (fiery) condiment for stirring back through the soup, to taste.

ENERGY	FAT	SAT FAT	PROTEIN	CARBS	SUGARS	SALT	FIBER
506kcal	17.9g	2.6g	17.3g	73g	13.9g	1.2g	13.6g

SHAKSHUKA, MY STYLE

CHIPPED POTATOES & SQUASH, PEPPERS & FIERY ROSE HARISSA

SERVES 4 | 30 MINUTES

7 oz potatoes

7 oz butternut squash

olive oil

3 mixed-color peppers

½ a bunch of fresh Italian parsley
   (½ oz)

2 cloves of garlic

1 teaspoon fennel seeds

1 teaspoon smoked paprika

1 teaspoon ground cumin

1 teaspoon rose harissa

1 x 14-oz can of quality plum
   tomatoes

4 large eggs

Scrub the potatoes and squash (seed, if needed), slice into ½-inch-thick chips, then place in a large non-stick frying pan on a medium heat with 1 tablespoon of oil. Seed and roughly chop the peppers, adding them to the pan as you go. Pick the parsley leaves, finely slicing the stalks. Peel and finely slice the garlic and add to the pan with the parsley stalks, fennel seeds, paprika and cumin, then cover and cook for 10 minutes, stirring regularly.

Flick over the harissa and scrunch in the tomatoes, then stir in ¼ of a can's worth of water, pop the lid back on and cook for a further 10 minutes, or until the potatoes and squash are soft, stirring occasionally. Remove the lid, stir in the parsley leaves and season with a pinch of sea salt, then cook until the sauce has thickened and reduced. Make 4 wells with the back of a spoon, crack in the eggs, pop the lid on and cook the eggs to your liking.

Nice served with warm flatbreads and extra harissa, if you like.

> I've made quite a dry shakshuka before, stirred through lots of beaten eggs and baked it to make a kind of frittata – very good it was, too!

ENERGY	FAT	SAT FAT	PROTEIN	CARBS	SUGARS	SALT	FIBER
219kcal	10.5g	2.2g	11.3g	22.5g	11.6g	0.8g	5.2g

SPEEDY EGG-FRIED RICE

LOADSA GREENS, ASIAN DRESSING, CHILI & SESAME SEEDS

SERVES 2 | 15 MINUTES

1 bok choy

7 oz delicate green veg, such as
   asparagus, sugar snap peas,
   baby spinach, peas

2 scallions

1 fresh red chili

¾-inch piece of fresh ginger

peanut oil

tamari

1 tablespoon white wine vinegar

1 x 8-oz package of ready-made
   basmati rice

1 lime

2 large eggs

1 tablespoon sesame seeds

2 sprigs of fresh cilantro

Place a large non-stick frying pan on a high heat. Halve the bok choy, then trim and prep the green veg, as necessary (snap off and discard the woody ends from the asparagus, if using, and halve the spears), and place in the pan. Trim, finely slice and add the scallions and chili, then peel, finely chop and add the ginger. Cook for 1 minute, or until lightly charred, tossing halfway, then drizzle in 2 tablespoons of oil, 1 tablespoon of tamari and the vinegar. Tip into a serving bowl.

Break up the rice and tip into the hot pan, finely grate in half the lime zest and add a splash of water. Stir-fry for 2 minutes, then flatten into an even layer. Beat and pour over the eggs, sprinkle with the sesame seeds and add a few drips of tamari, then cover and turn the heat off. Leave for 2 minutes (the residual heat will cook the egg), then serve with the veg, tearing over the cilantro leaves. Cut the lime into wedges for squeezing over.

> Obviously you can cook your own rice and simply refresh under cold water and drain, but using the packages is a great little cheat if you're short on time.

ENERGY	FAT	SAT FAT	PROTEIN	CARBS	SUGARS	SALT	FIBER
426kcal	22.3g	4.9g	17.4g	41.3g	3.9g	1.2g	4.6g

BRUNCH

AUSSIE-STYLE BRUNCH BOWLS

AVO, EGGS, SPROUTS & VEG, INCREDIBLE APRICOT, CHILI & TOMATO DRESSING

SERVES 4 | 15 MINUTES

4 large eggs

3 oz podded fava beans

3 oz baby spinach

3 oz mixed sprouts

1½ oz mixed seeds

½ an English cucumber

1 ripe beefsteak tomato

1 ripe avocado

1½ oz shelled unsalted walnut
halves

1 bunch of mixed fresh herbs,
such as cilantro, Italian parsley,
mint (1 oz)

1 bunch of radishes, ideally
with leaves

1 fresh red chili

8 dried apricots

8 ripe mixed-color cherry
tomatoes

extra virgin olive oil

½ a lemon

Soft-boil the eggs in a pan of boiling water on a medium-high heat for 5½ minutes, then drain, cool under cold running water and peel. Meanwhile, get all the veg prepped, dividing it between 4 bowls in little piles as you go: lightly crack the fava beans in a pestle and mortar, and place in the bowls with the spinach, sprouts and seeds. Chop the cucumber, slice the tomato, quarter, pit and peel the avocado, bash the walnuts and pick most of the herb leaves, then arrange nicely in the bowls along with the radishes, halving and adding the eggs.

For the dressing, roughly chop the chili (seed, if you like), then bash to a paste in a pestle and mortar with the remaining herb leaves. Roughly chop and bash in the apricots, followed by the cherry tomatoes — you may need to work in batches. Muddle in 3 tablespoons of oil and the lemon juice, season to taste with sea salt and black pepper, then transfer to 4 little bowls.

Pour over the dressing and toss together, then serve with bread or toast.

> For me, this dish is all about ducking and diving around the seasons, having fun and not being boring, so change up the veggies and nuts and make your mark.

ENERGY	FAT	SAT FAT	PROTEIN	CARBS	SUGARS	SALT	FIBER
437kcal	34.2g	5.7g	17.5g	18g	13.6g	0.3g	5.9g

HONEYED HALLOUMI, FIGS & FLATBREADS

CHOPPED SALAD, YOGURT, TAHINI, SOFT-BOILED EGGS & DUKKAH

SERVES 4 | 20 MINUTES

4 large eggs

1 gem lettuce

4 sprigs of fresh mint

1 ripe beefsteak tomato

½ an English cucumber

2 tablespoons plain yogurt

2 tablespoons tahini

1 lemon

7½ oz halloumi cheese

olive oil

2 tablespoons sesame seeds

4 teaspoons liquid honey

4 ripe figs

8 black olives (with pits)

1 tablespoon dukkah

4 flatbreads

Soft-boil the eggs in a pan of boiling water on a medium-high heat for 5½ minutes, then drain, cool under cold running water and peel. Trim the lettuce and pick the mint leaves, then chop with the tomato and cucumber. Drizzle over the yogurt and tahini, squeeze over the lemon juice, then continue chopping and mixing until fine. Season to taste with sea salt and black pepper.

Slice the halloumi lengthways into 4, then place in a large non-stick frying pan on a medium heat with 1 tablespoon of oil. Cook for 2 minutes on each side, scatter in the sesame seeds and press and turn to coat all over. Remove to a plate, then drizzle with the honey. Quarter the figs, pit the olives, then halve the eggs and sprinkle with the dukkah. Serve with warm flatbreads and display like a picnic.

You can add to this salad in so many ways, with interesting grains, salads, salsas or fruit – it's all about choice, contrast and variety. Delicious!

ENERGY	FAT	SAT FAT	PROTEIN	CARBS	SUGARS	SALT	FIBER
536kcal	33.4g	13.2g	28.2g	31.1g	14.3g	2.5g	4g

SUPER SPINACH PANCAKES

AVOCADO, TOMATO, COTTAGE CHEESE, CHILI & CILANTRO

SERVES 6 | 25 MINUTES

1 ripe avocado

12 oz ripe mixed-color cherry tomatoes

3½ oz baby spinach

3 scallions

½ a bunch of fresh cilantro (½ oz)

1 lime

extra virgin olive oil

1 large egg

1 cup self-rising flour

1 cup reduced-fat (2%) milk

olive oil

10 oz cottage cheese

hot chili sauce

Halve, pit, peel and finely slice the avocado and quarter the tomatoes, then place in a salad bowl with a quarter of the spinach. Trim, finely slice and add the scallions and pick in the cilantro leaves, then squeeze over the lime juice. Drizzle with 1 tablespoon of extra virgin olive oil, season to perfection with sea salt and black pepper, toss to coat and put aside.

Crack the egg into a blender, add the flour, milk, remaining spinach and a pinch of pepper, then blitz until smooth. Place a large non-stick frying pan on a medium heat, rub the pan with a little olive oil, then pour in a thin layer of batter, swirling it up and around the edges. Cook on one side only for 2 minutes, or until lightly golden, then stack up on a serving plate and repeat.

Top each pancake with dollops of cottage cheese, the avocado salad, and a few good shakes of chili sauce. Really nice served with extra lime wedges for squeezing over, and a fried egg on top, if you fancy.

> Instead of spinach you could use a mixture of soft herbs, such as parsley, mint, basil or tarragon – whatever you like!

ENERGY	FAT	SAT FAT	PROTEIN	CARBS	SUGARS	SALT	FIBER
331kcal	13.3g	4g	13.5g	42.3g	6.3g	1.2g	3g

BRUNCH-STYLE EGG CURRY

FLUFFY YOGURT FLATBREADS, CILANTRO, LEMON & FRESH CHILI

SERVES 6 | 30 MINUTES

2 onions

2 cloves of garlic

¾-inch piece of fresh ginger

2 fresh red chilies

olive oil

2 tablespoons korma curry paste

9 large eggs

1 x 14-oz can of quality plum tomatoes

1 x 14-oz can of light coconut milk

1⅓ cups self-rising flour, plus extra for dusting

⅔ cup plain yogurt

½ a bunch of fresh cilantro (½ oz)

1 lemon

Peel and finely slice the onions, garlic and ginger, finely slice 1 of the chilies, then place in a large casserole pan on a high heat with 1 tablespoon of oil. Fry for 10 minutes, or until soft, stirring constantly. Stir in the paste, then cook for a further 5 minutes, or until sticky and lightly caramelized, stirring regularly. Meanwhile, cook the eggs in a pan of boiling water on a medium-high heat for 7 minutes, then drain, cool under cold running water and peel.

Scrunch the tomatoes into the pan, and pour in the coconut milk. Simmer on a low heat for 10 minutes, stirring occasionally, halving and adding the eggs for the last 5 minutes. Meanwhile, put the flour, yogurt, 2 tablespoons of oil and a pinch of sea salt into a bowl, then mix, bring together and pat into a dough. Halve, then roll out each piece on a flour-dusted surface until just under ½ inch thick. One at a time, cook in a large non-stick frying pan on a medium heat for 3 minutes, or until golden and cooked through, turning halfway.

Pick and finely chop the cilantro leaves, stir into the curry, then season to taste. Tear and divide up the flatbreads, and top with a spoon of curry. Finely slice and scatter over the remaining chili, and slice the lemon into wedges for squeezing over. Tasty served with an extra dollop of yogurt, if you like.

> You can embellish this curry by adding paneer, chickpeas or even lima beans — they will give it a sumptuous, comforting feel. And if you fancy rice instead of bread, happy days!

ENERGY	FAT	SAT FAT	PROTEIN	CARBS	SUGARS	SALT	FIBER
415kcal	22.7g	7.8g	17.1g	37.2g	10.2g	1.7g	3.6g

VEGGIE FRY-UP

CRISPY POLENTA, JALAPEÑO SALSA, FRIED EGGS, MUSHROOMS & AVOCADO

SERVES 4 | 40 MINUTES PLUS SETTING

5 oz quick-cook polenta

¾ oz Parmesan cheese

olive oil

1 x 8-oz jar of pickled jalapeño chilies

1 bunch of fresh cilantro (1 oz)

1 x 14-oz can of quality plum tomatoes

7 oz mixed mushrooms

1 ripe avocado

1 lime

4 large eggs

Cook the polenta in a pan of boiling salted water according to the package instructions, whisking constantly to prevent lumps. It's ready when it comes easily away from the edge of the pan – you want a thick consistency. Remove from the heat, then grate in and stir through the Parmesan. Tip into a 8- x 6-inch oiled baking dish (so it's 1 inch thick), forking up the top to give great texture. Leave to set.

Tip the jalapeños (juices and all) into a blender, then add the cilantro (stalks and all) and whiz until fine. Pour back into the jar – this will keep in the fridge for a couple of weeks for jazzing up future meals. Tip the tomatoes into a small pan, mashing them with a potato masher until fairly smooth, then season to taste and leave to blip away over a medium heat. Once the polenta is set, cut into 4 chunky wedges and place in a large non-stick frying pan over a medium heat with 1 tablespoon of oil. Once dark golden on one side, flip the polenta over, add the mushrooms to the gaps in the pan, and turn occasionally until softened.

Halve, pit, peel and finely slice the avocado, then squeeze over the lime juice. Spoon the tomato sauce onto plates, add the polenta wedges and mushrooms, then fry the eggs to your liking and place on top. Drizzle over a little jalapeño salsa, to taste, then add the avocado and get stuck in.

Sometimes I embellish this dish by adding baby spinach with the avocado, and crumbling over some feta.

To make vegetarian: swap Parmesan for vegetarian hard cheese.

ENERGY	FAT	SAT FAT	PROTEIN	CARBS	SUGARS	SALT	FIBER
340kcal	16.4g	4.4g	14g	34.5g	4.4g	1.2g	2.5g

ZUCCHINI & FETA SCONES

JAZZED-UP FRIED EGGS, TOMATOES, MINT & CHILI

SERVES 2 + 12 LEFTOVER SCONES | 45 MINUTES PLUS CHILLING

1 lb zucchini

3⅓ cups self-rising flour

2 level teaspoons baking powder

11 tablespoons unsalted butter (cold)

2 teaspoons dried chili flakes

7 oz feta cheese

4 large eggs

1 fresh red chili

olive oil

4 sprigs of fresh mint

5 oz ripe mixed-color cherry tomatoes

Preheat the oven to 400°F. Coarsely grate the zucchini (discard the seedy core), then place in a large bowl with a pinch of sea salt. Scrunch and squeeze together, then leave aside. Meanwhile, tip the flour into a bowl with the baking powder, then chop and rub in the butter. Squeeze the zucchini hard to get rid of any excess water, then stir through the flour mixture with the chili flakes, and crumble in the feta. Make a well in the middle, crack in 2 of the eggs, then mix, pat and bring together into a dough (don't overwork it for a crumbly texture). Wrap in plastic wrap and chill in the fridge for 15 minutes.

Roll out the chilled dough on a floured surface until 1¼ inches thick, then stamp out the scones using a 2½-inch cutter. Place on a lined baking sheet and bake for 20 minutes, or until golden, then leave to cool. Meanwhile, very finely slice the chili. Drizzle 1 tablespoon of oil into a large non-stick frying pan on a medium heat, add half the chili in the middle and pick in half the mint leaves, then crack an egg over the top. Scatter half the tomatoes in and around the edge of the pan, cover with a lid and cook for 2 minutes, or until cooked to your liking, then serve and repeat.

Nice served with a cup of builder's or mint tea.

> Extra scones can be frozen raw, then cooked to order straight from frozen at 350°F for 35 minutes.

ENERGY	FAT	SAT FAT	PROTEIN	CARBS	SUGARS	SALT	FIBER
411kcal	26.3g	10.5g	15.1g	31.3g	4g	1.6g	1.9g

AVOCADO & JALAPEÑO HASH BROWN

ROASTED VINE TOMATOES, SCALLIONS, CILANTRO & POACHED EGGS

SERVES 4 | 35 MINUTES

8 oz ripe cherry tomatoes,
  on the vine

olive oil

1¾ lbs Yukon Gold potatoes

4 scallions

2 fresh jalapeño chilies

1 ripe avocado

¾ oz Parmesan cheese

4 large eggs

4 sprigs of fresh cilantro

1 lime

Preheat the oven to 375°F. Place the tomatoes on a baking sheet, drizzle with 1 tablespoon of oil, season with sea salt and black pepper, then roast for 30 minutes. Meanwhile, scrub and coarsely grate the potatoes, then squeeze dry in a clean kitchen towel. Place a large non-stick ovenproof frying pan on a medium heat. Roughly slice the scallions and jalapeños (seed, if you like), and halve, pit, peel and finely slice the avocado. Mix everything together, then place in the pan with 1 tablespoon of oil and cook for 5 minutes, stirring occasionally. Finely grate in half the Parmesan and season with salt and pepper, then pat and flatten everything down into an even layer. Cook for 10 minutes, or until golden and crisp on the bottom, then transfer to the oven for a final 10 minutes.

Meanwhile, poach the eggs to your liking. Turn the hash brown out onto a board (it's the perfect combo of soft and crispy), then finely grate over the remaining Parmesan. Divide between plates, top with the tomatoes and poached eggs, then tear over the cilantro leaves. Serve with lime wedges for squeezing over.

> Cooked avocado is utterly delicious – however, it does divide people. If you're not a fan, simply leave it out of the hash brown and serve it fresh on top.

To make vegetarian: swap Parmesan for vegetarian hard cheese.

ENERGY	FAT	SAT FAT	PROTEIN	CARBS	SUGARS	SALT	FIBER
377kcal	19.9g	4.6g	14.4g	38.1g	4.3g	1.3g	3.6g

COMFORTING CONGEE BOWL

SOFT-BOILED EGGS, SHIITAKE BACON, CHILI & SHREDDED SCALLION

SERVES 4 | 1 HOUR

4 cloves of garlic

1½-inch piece of fresh ginger

1⅓ cups jasmine rice

6 cups vegetable stock

1 star anise

8 oz shiitake mushrooms

peanut oil

4 large eggs

2 scallions

1 fresh red chili

2 sprigs of fresh cilantro

1 tablespoon black sesame seeds

reduced-sodium soy sauce

Preheat the oven to 400°F. Peel the garlic and ginger, bash to a paste in a pestle and mortar, and scrape into a large pan on a medium heat. Add the rice, vegetable stock, 2 cups of water, the star anise and a pinch of sea salt and black pepper. Bring to a boil, then simmer on a low heat for 45 minutes, or until it resembles a porridge consistency, beating with a wooden spoon as it starts to thicken, and loosening with a splash of water, if needed.

With 30 minutes to go, trim and very finely slice the mushrooms. Toss with 1 tablespoon of oil and a small pinch of salt and pepper, then spread out in a single layer over a couple of oiled baking sheets. Roast for 20 minutes, or until golden and perfectly crisp (the flavor and snappy texture are just incredible).

Meanwhile, soft-boil the eggs in a pan of boiling water on a medium-high heat for 5½ minutes, drain, cool under cold running water, then peel and halve. Trim and finely shred the scallions, finely slice the chili, and pick the cilantro leaves. Divide the congee between warm bowls, discarding the star anise. Top each with an egg, mushrooms, scallions, chili and cilantro, and scatter over the sesame seeds. Serve drizzled with soy, to taste.

> Hot, comforting congee is particularly good with a quick pickle, made by scrunching shredded carrot and cabbage with a little rice wine vinegar.

ENERGY	FAT	SAT FAT	PROTEIN	CARBS	SUGARS	SALT	FIBER
394kcal	12.4g	2.7g	17.3g	58.1g	2g	1g	2.4g

SPEEDY SPICED POCKET BREAD

SOFT-COOKED EGG, FETA & PEAS, CHUNKY TOMATO SALSA

SERVES 1 | 10 MINUTES

¼ of a red onion

1 fresh green or yellow chili

1 large whole-wheat tortilla

1 large egg

½ oz feta cheese

1 oz fresh or frozen peas

curry powder

3½ oz ripe mixed-color
   cherry tomatoes

¼-inch piece of fresh ginger

extra virgin olive oil

1 lime

2 sprigs of fresh cilantro

1 tablespoon plain yogurt

Peel the onion and very finely slice with the chili. Lay the tortilla flat, crack the egg on top, then gently move the yolk around with your fingers (without breaking it) to spread the white to the edges, ending up with the yolk back in the middle. Crumble the feta over one half, then scatter the onion, chili and peas over the feta. Dust with ½ a teaspoon of curry powder, then fold in half. Carefully transfer to a large non-stick frying pan on a medium-low heat, and cook for 3 minutes on each side for a soft, runny egg – cook for longer, if you prefer.

Meanwhile, finely grate 2 tomatoes into a bowl. Peel and finely grate in the ginger, drizzle in 1 teaspoon of oil, then quarter and stir through the remaining tomatoes. Squeeze over half the lime juice, then mix and season to perfection with sea salt and black pepper. Pick and stir through the cilantro leaves.

Cut or tear the sandwich in half, and serve with the tomato salsa, yogurt, a flick of curry powder and an extra squeeze of lime juice.

> A brilliantly flexible dish for the whole family – feel free to halt the chili and curry powder if making for little ones, or indeed to ramp up the heat if (like me!) you're a bit of a chili fiend.

ENERGY	FAT	SAT FAT	PROTEIN	CARBS	SUGARS	SALT	FIBER
389kcal	16.7g	6g	19.7g	39g	10.3g	1.2g	9g

BEAUTIFUL BUCKWHEAT PANCAKES

ROASTED RHUBARB & PLUMS, CREAMY YOGURT & BASHED HAZELNUTS

SERVES 4 | 30 MINUTES

2 large eggs

1 cup + 2 tablespoons
buckwheat flour

1¼ cups reduced-fat (2%) milk

10 oz rhubarb

8 ripe plums

2 blood or regular oranges

¼ cup liquid honey

1 sprig of fresh rosemary

1½ oz blanched hazelnuts

unsalted butter

4 heaping tablespoons plain
Greek yogurt

Preheat the oven to 350°F. Crack the eggs into a bowl, add the flour, milk and a pinch of sea salt, whisk until smooth, then chill until needed.

Trim the rhubarb, slice into 1½-inch pieces and place in a 14- x 10-inch baking dish. Halve and pit the plums, then place cut-side up in the dish. Finely grate over the orange zest, squeeze over the juice, then drizzle with the honey. Add the rosemary sprig to the dish (this will add a delicious subtle perfume) and roast for 30 minutes, or until softened and starting to caramelize.

Lightly bash the nuts in a pestle and mortar, then toast in a large dry non-stick frying pan on a medium heat until golden, and tip into a bowl. Place the pan back on the heat, and rub with a little butter. Loosen the batter with a splash of water, if needed, then pour in a ladleful, swirling it up and around the edges of the pan. Cook until lightly golden on both sides, then slide onto a plate. Serve as and when ready, with a dollop of yogurt, a quarter of the fruit, a scattering of nuts and a drizzle of juice from the fruit dish, then repeat. What a treat!

> The buckwheat flour will give you a really interesting flavor, but feel free to use regular whole-wheat flour, if you prefer.

ENERGY	FAT	SAT FAT	PROTEIN	CARBS	SUGARS	SALT	FIBER
446kcal	15.8g	4.7g	15.8g	62.9g	33.8g	0.8g	4.9g

RIPPLED SMOOTHIE BOWLS
CRUNCHY GRANOLA, BLUEBERRY COMPOTE, LIME-SPIKED BANANA

SERVES 4 | 25 MINUTES

1¾ oz mixed unsalted nuts
 and seeds

1½ cups large-flake rolled oats

olive oil

liquid honey

1 tablespoon unsweetened
 shredded, dried or desiccated
 coconut, plus extra to serve

10 oz frozen blueberries

3 ripe bananas

1¼ cups plain yogurt

1 teaspoon vanilla bean paste

½ a lime

Preheat the oven to 350°F. Roughly chop the nuts and seeds, then place in a large bowl with half the oats. Drizzle in ½ a tablespoon each of oil and honey, then mix well. Spread out evenly on a lined baking sheet and roast for 20 minutes, or until lightly golden, then remove and stir through the coconut.

Meanwhile, heat the blueberries and ½ a tablespoon of honey in a small pan on a medium heat for 5 minutes, stirring occasionally and adding a splash of water to loosen, if needed. Peel two of the bananas, then whiz in a blender with the yogurt, vanilla and the remaining oats until smooth. Divide three-quarters of the smoothie between 4 shallow bowls, then add half the blueberry compote to the blender and whiz again. Ripple into the bowls, then spoon over the remaining compote. Peel and slice the remaining banana, toss with the lime juice, then add to the bowl with the warm granola and an extra pinch of coconut.

I always peel, chop and freeze bananas that are on the turn – frozen bananas will give you a slightly thicker and more refreshing result.

ENERGY	FAT	SAT FAT	PROTEIN	CARBS	SUGARS	SALT	FIBER
409kcal	14.9g	4.3g	12.1g	60.3g	30.8g	0.1g	5.5g

STICKY TOFFEE WAFFLES

CARAMELIZED BANANAS, CREAMY YOGURT, FLAKED ALMONDS & POMEGRANATE

SERVES 4 | 30 MINUTES

1 cup whole-wheat self-rising flour

1 teaspoon baking powder

1 teaspoon ground cinnamon

4 Medjool dates

3 ripe bananas

2 large eggs

1 cup reduced-fat (2%) milk

olive oil

¾ oz flaked almonds

2 tablespoons maple syrup

½ a pomegranate

¼ cup plain yogurt

Place the flour, baking powder, cinnamon and dates in a blender. Peel and add 1 banana, then crack in the eggs, pour in the milk and whiz to a thick, smooth batter. Get your waffle machine switched on and ready to go, rubbing it with a little oil. Once super-hot, ladle in the batter and seal, following the machine instructions until the waffles are golden and cooked through (usually around 7 minutes), then repeat. Waffle machines vary slightly – both in size and temperature – so you'll need to use your instincts and adjust accordingly.

Meanwhile, toast the almonds in a dry non-stick frying pan on a medium heat until lightly golden, then tip into a bowl, placing the pan back on the heat. Peel and slice the remaining bananas ½ inch thick, then place in the pan with the maple syrup. Cook gently until golden and caramelized, turning to coat. Holding the pomegranate half cut-side down, bash the back of it with a spoon so all the seeds come tumbling out. Place each cooked waffle on a plate, dollop with yogurt, then top with the caramelized banana, toasted almonds and pomegranate seeds.

> Unsurprisingly, these waffles are delicious served with chocolate – use a fine grater and you'll find that a little goes a long way but looks and tastes amazing!

ENERGY	FAT	SAT FAT	PROTEIN	CARBS	SUGARS	SALT	FIBER
342kcal	9.6g	2.6g	13.8g	54.4g	25.1g	0.5g	5.7g

FRIDAY NIGHT NIBBLES

BRILLIANT BANG BANG CUCUMBER

TOASTED SESAME SEEDS, SOY, CHILI FLAKES & LIP-SMACKING SZECHUAN PEPPER

SERVES 4 | 10 MINUTES

1 large English cucumber

½–1 teaspoon dried chili flakes

½–1 teaspoon Szechuan pepper

2 tablespoons sesame seeds

2 tablespoons reduced-sodium
soy sauce

2 tablespoons black rice or
balsamic vinegar

1 teaspoon sesame oil

Scratch the outside of the cucumber with a fork to create grooves. With your fist, "bang bang" the cucumber flat, then roughly slice up and place in a bowl with a really good pinch of sea salt. Scrunch up aggressively and leave for 5 minutes.

Bash the chili flakes and Szechuan pepper in a pestle and mortar until fine, then muddle in and lightly crack the sesame seeds. Tip into a dry non-stick frying pan and toast on a medium heat until beautifully golden, tossing regularly.

Grab the cucumber with your hands and squeeze hard to remove any salty liquid, then transfer to a serving bowl. Drizzle with the soy, vinegar and oil, then scrunch together and sprinkle over the hot sizzling seeds.

Wonderful with simple crisps and your favorite beer or spirit.

> This method is also brilliant with bashed-up carrots (use a rolling pin), daikon or radish. Love it!

ENERGY	FAT	SAT FAT	PROTEIN	CARBS	SUGARS	SALT	FIBER
56kcal	3.9g	0.5g	2.8g	2.8g	2.2g	1.3g	1.1g

CHEESY KIMCHI TOASTIE

EPIC BRITTLE CRUNCHY CHEESE CROWN

SERVES 1 | 10 MINUTES

2 slices of soft bread

1½ oz sharp Cheddar cheese

1½ oz quality kimchi

Place one piece of bread on a board and grate over a third of the cheese. Finely chop the kimchi and spread it over the cheese, right to the edges of the bread, then grate over half the remaining cheese. Place the second piece of bread on top, then transfer to a large non-stick frying pan on a medium heat. Cook for 2 minutes on each side, or until beautifully golden, then remove from the pan. Grate the remaining cheese and scatter over the surface of the pan, then place the toastie back on top. After around 30 seconds (or when the cheese is nicely golden), confidently lift the toastie up using a slotted spatula – the cheese from the sides will hang down and harden after about 20 seconds – then carefully turn it over to reveal your handsome cheese crown.

Of course you can serve this for one, but I usually cut it up into soldiers and share it as more of a nibble, with a cold beer.

Sometimes I serve this with a little bowl of finely bashed unsalted nuts, and dip the cheesy exposed sides for extra flavor and crunch.

ENERGY	FAT	SAT FAT	PROTEIN	CARBS	SUGARS	SALT	FIBER
352kcal	15.5g	8.6g	17.4g	37.5g	2.6g	1.9g	2.8g

GO-TO HUMMUS

LOTS OF DELICIOUS WAYS

SERVES 6 | 5 MINUTES PLUS TOPPINGS

1 x 15-oz can of chickpeas

2 tablespoons tahini

½ a clove of garlic

½ a lemon

extra virgin olive oil

4 sprigs of fresh Italian parsley

smoked paprika

Drain the chickpeas and tip into a blender with the tahini. Peel and add the garlic, squeeze in the lemon juice and drizzle in ¼ cup of oil, then whiz until super-smooth or still with texture, depending on your preference. Loosen with a splash of water, if needed. Season to taste with sea salt and black pepper, then transfer to a plate or bowl. This is my basic go-to hummus – it's the plate at the bottom of the picture. To garnish, pick, finely chop and add the parsley in 4 little pinches, alternating with pinches of smoked paprika.

Traveling clockwise in the picture is **go-to hummus** with a decent dollop of **harissa** swirled into the middle. Simply delicious!

Above that: it's quite nice to hold back some whole chickpeas when making the **go-to hummus**, then simply dress with **lemon juice** and **extra virgin olive oil**, place on top, and finish with a good spoonful of **tahini**.

And last but not least: **go-to hummus** topped with crispy black beans. Drain ½ a 15-oz can of **black beans** and fry until popped and crispy, then add ½ a tablespoon of **extra virgin olive oil** and ½ a teaspoon of **smoked paprika**. Serve topped with finely chopped **parsley** and an extra pinch or two of paprika, sprinkled from a height. Yum!

Whichever option you choose, finish with a drizzle of extra virgin olive oil.

If you can make the hummus using jarred chickpeas (super-tasty juices and all), they're normally bigger and creamier, and the flavor and texture are phenomenal – it's worth searching them out!

ENERGY	FAT	SAT FAT	PROTEIN	CARBS	SUGARS	SALT	FIBER
146kcal	11.8g	1.7g	3.6g	6.3g	0.3g	0g	2.3g

CRISPY TORN TACOS

SMASHED SWEET POTATO, APPLE & CHILI SALSA

MAKES 4 | **1 HOUR 15 MINUTES**

1 large sweet potato (10 oz)

1 teaspoon smoked paprika

2 limes

1 ripe tomato

¼ of a red onion

4 sprigs of fresh mint

½ an eating apple

½ a fresh red chili

1 large flour tortilla

Preheat the oven to 350°F. Scrub the sweet potato, dust with smoked paprika, and roast for 1 hour, or until tender. Meanwhile, squeeze the lime juice into a bowl. Seed the tomato, peel the onion and pick the mint leaves, then very finely chop with the apple and chili, and stir into the bowl.

Pinch off and reserve the sweet potato skin. Tear the tortilla into quarters, then rack up between the domes of an upside-down muffin pan, which will hold the tortillas in shape (they'll be a bit irregular, but it's all part of the charm). Bake for 10 minutes, or until golden and crisp, tearing the sweet potato skin onto the pan for the last 5 minutes. Mash the sweet potato and season to taste with sea salt and black pepper, then divide between the hot taco shells and top with the zingy apple and chili salsa, and the crispy skin. Serve with a cold beer – what a treat!

> Feel free to fill the taco shells with other mashed veg – squash, carrots and purple potatoes are all super-tasty.

ENERGY	FAT	SAT FAT	PROTEIN	CARBS	SUGARS	SALT	FIBER
127kcal	1.3g	0.5g	2.6g	28g	7.9g	0.3g	1.4g

POLENTA CHIPS

CRISPY ROSEMARY & PARMESAN

SERVES 8 | I HOUR 30 MINUTES PLUS SETTING

14 oz quick-cook polenta

1½ oz Parmesan cheese

olive oil

4 sprigs of fresh rosemary

Cook the polenta in a pan of boiling salted water according to the package instructions, whisking constantly to prevent lumps. It's ready when it comes easily away from the edge of the pan – you want a thick consistency. Remove from the heat, grate in and stir through half the Parmesan, then tip onto an oiled baking pan, forking up the top to give great texture. Leave to set.

Preheat the oven to 350°F. Tear or cut the polenta into chips or chunky wedges, toss with a little oil, then spread out in a single layer on a couple of large non-stick baking sheets. Roast for 50 minutes, or until beautifully golden and crisp, turning them and picking over the rosemary leaves for the last 10 minutes. Finely grate over the remaining Parmesan, then get stuck in.

Although I love the simplicity of the flavors here, you can add pungent things, such as tapenade, pastes, pesto or chopped herbs, to the polenta before setting, if you like.

To make vegetarian: swap Parmesan for vegetarian hard cheese.

ENERGY	FAT	SAT FAT	PROTEIN	CARBS	SUGARS	SALT	FIBER
236kcal	5.9g	1.8g	5.3g	39.9g	0.3g	0.2g	1.6g

TORTILLA CHIPS & DIPS

CHILI & TOMATO, CHEESE, SCALLION & LIME

SERVES 2 | 15 MINUTES

2 scallions

2 tablespoons light cream cheese

1 lime

2 large flour tortillas

1 fresh red chili

3½ oz ripe cherry tomatoes

olive oil

2 sprigs of fresh cilantro

Trim and finely slice the scallions and mix with the cream cheese, half the lime juice and a splash of water to give you a nice consistency. Roughly slice the tortillas and place in a large dry non-stick frying pan on a medium heat, ideally in one layer. Turn regularly until golden and crisp, then tip onto a plate.

Meanwhile, finely slice the chili, quarter the tomatoes and season with sea salt and black pepper. Drizzle 1 tablespoon of oil into the pan, place back on a medium heat, add the chili and tomatoes and squeeze over the remaining lime juice. Stir vigorously for 1 minute, then tip over the crispy tortillas. Dollop the creamy dip on top, and pick over the cilantro leaves.

Serve with your favorite beer or a glass of chilled white wine.

> Smashed avo or a handful of warmed black beans and grated Cheddar make tasty topping alternatives.

ENERGY	FAT	SAT FAT	PROTEIN	CARBS	SUGARS	SALT	FIBER
243kcal	7.3g	3.8g	8.1g	38.5g	5.2g	1.8g	3.3g

PLOUGHMAN'S NACHOS

FLAVORED BUTTER, MELTY CHEESE & ZINGY PICKLED ONIONS

SERVES 6 | 15 MINUTES

¼ cup unsalted butter (at room temperature)

1 tablespoon HP sauce

½ a loaf of seeded bread

2 oz sharp Cheddar cheese

6 pickled onions

Preheat the oven to 350°F. Fork up the butter and beat with the HP sauce. Slice the bread as finely as you can, spread with the flavored butter, and place on a couple of large baking sheets in a single layer. Very finely grate over the Cheddar, then bake for 10 minutes, or until golden and crisp. Finely slice the pickled onions and separate into rings, then scatter over the hot toasts.

Delicious served with sliced apple and a glass of chilled cider.

> Smashed up, these tasty bites make particularly good croutons for soup, or form the base of a fantastic ploughman's salad with crunchy lettuce and sprouting cress.

ENERGY	FAT	SAT FAT	PROTEIN	CARBS	SUGARS	SALT	FIBER
302kcal	16.7g	8g	9.4g	30.7g	3.7g	1g	4.4g

SIMPLE PICKLE

BEAUTIFUL SEASONAL VEG, COMPLEMENTARY HERBS & SPICES

MAKES 1 LARGE JAR | 15 MINUTES

2 cups mineral water

2 cups cider vinegar

1 lb vegetables, such as carrots,
   artichokes, radishes,
   cucumber, celery, mixed
   beans, asparagus, cauliflower,
   broccoli, beets

a few sprigs of fresh herbs, such
   as rosemary, thyme, bay,
   tarragon, fennel, marjoram

1 teaspoon spices, such as
   mustard seeds, cardamom,
   fennel seeds, cumin seeds,
   dried chili, saffron

optional: fragrant ingredients,
   such as garlic, fresh chili,
   turmeric, ginger, horseradish

This is a brilliant general pickle that gives you a structure to rely on, but also some flexibility with vegetables, spices and flavorings, to allow your creativity to come out – tweak to perfection as you experiment with new combinations.

Tip the water, vinegar and 2 tablespoons of sea salt into a large pan and bring to a simmer. Select the vegetable(s) you'd like to use, then wash and prep to an agreeable bite size. Add to the pan with your chosen herb and spice combination, and any additional fragrant ingredients, to taste (if using), then bring to a boil and poach until half cooked (there's no need to poach salad veg, such as cucumber, first), to keep a good crunch. Decant the veg and liquor into a sterilized jar and secure the lid – good to eat after a day or two, and if all is sterilized well (see below), they'll be good for 3 months unopened and kept in a dark place. Once opened, leave in the fridge and use within a week or two. If you choose not to sterilize, they'll keep happily in the fridge for up to 2 weeks.

How to sterilize: simply boil the jar, lid and any utensils used to fill the jar for 15 minutes, making sure not to use any unsterile items until after you've sealed the jar.

These values are based on 100g.

ENERGY	FAT	SAT FAT	PROTEIN	CARBS	SUGARS	SALT	FIBER
26kcal	0.5g	0.1g	2g	4g	2.5g	0.3g	2g

SUPERCHARGED BABA GANOUSH

SMOKY EGGPLANT, TAHINI, FETA, LETTUCE CUPS & POMEGRANATE

SERVES 10 | 50 MINUTES

3 large eggplants (14 oz each)

3 tablespoons tahini

1 lemon

¼ of a clove of garlic

extra virgin olive oil

1½ oz feta cheese

1 teaspoon rose harissa

1 bunch of fresh Italian parsley (1 oz)

1 teaspoon liquid honey

4 mixed-color endive

2 little gem lettuces

½ a pomegranate

Char the eggplants on a grill pan, under the broiler (prick them first!), over a gas flame or on a barbecue for 25 minutes, or until blackened all over and soft inside. Meanwhile, put the tahini (or use peanut or almond butter) into a bowl, finely grate in the lemon zest and squeeze in the juice. Peel and finely grate in the garlic, muddle in 2 tablespoons of oil and crumble in most of the feta.

Halve the eggplants and scoop the soft flesh into the bowl, discarding the blackened skins. Add the harissa and beat together to the consistency you like. Finely chop the parsley (stalks and all) and stir into the bowl with the honey. Taste and season to perfection with sea salt and black pepper.

Trim the endive and lettuce, click the leaves apart and arrange on a platter, placing the baba ganoush in the center. Hold the pomegranate half cut-side down, bash the back of it with a spoon so all the seeds tumble out, then scatter over the platter, and crumble over the remaining feta.

Nice with a glass of chilled rosé.

> Halved or quartered grapes also work well instead of pomegranate, if you prefer.

ENERGY	FAT	SAT FAT	PROTEIN	CARBS	SUGARS	SALT	FIBER
113kcal	6.6g	1.4g	3.6g	10.7g	7.2g	0.2g	1.1g

SPEEDY DOUGH BALLS

SMOKIN' SWEET PEPPER & CHILI RIPPLED CREAM CHEESE DIP

SERVES 4–6 | 20 MINUTES

1⅔ cups self-rising flour

olive oil

1 x 9-oz jar of roasted peppers in brine

1 fresh red chili

½ teaspoon sweet smoked paprika

3½ oz light cream cheese

Place the flour in a bowl, make a well in the middle, then mix in around ⅔ cup of water and bring together to form a dough. Knead vigorously for a few minutes, then roll out into a long sausage, roughly ¾ inch thick. Chop into ¾-inch nuggets, toss in 2 tablespoons of oil, then rest for 5 minutes. Place in a non-stick frying pan over a medium heat for around 10 minutes, or until golden and cooked through, turning occasionally.

Place the peppers (juices and all), chili and paprika in a food processor and blitz until smooth. Beat the cream cheese in a bowl, then fold and swirl through a quarter of the pepper sauce. Tip the rest back into the jar and save in the fridge for future meals (amazing used to flavor rice or couscous).

Serve the dough balls topped with the dip – delicious with a glass of chilled rosé.

> Sometimes I flavor the dough with a little crumbled cheese and chopped herbs.

ENERGY	FAT	SAT FAT	PROTEIN	CARBS	SUGARS	SALT	FIBER
317kcal	10.2g	2.9g	8g	51.1g	4.3g	1.3g	2.8g

CRUNCHY SUMMER ROLLS

CRISP GRATED VEG, APPLE, CHILI & MINT, PEANUT DIP

SERVES 4 (MAKES 8) | **30 MINUTES**

3 ½ oz vermicelli rice noodles

sesame oil

3 teaspoons reduced-sodium
   soy sauce

3 carrots

1 bunch of radishes

1 eating apple

2 limes

1 fresh red chili

1 mixed bunch of fresh mint
   and cilantro (1 oz)

1 cup sprouting cress

8 rice paper wrappers

2 heaping tablespoons crunchy
   peanut butter

Cook the noodles according to the package instructions, then drain and refresh under cold running water. Drizzle over 1 tablespoon of oil and 1 teaspoon of soy sauce. Scrub the carrots and coarsely grate with the radishes and apple, and squeeze over the juice of ½ a lime. Finely slice the chili, pick the herb leaves and snip the cress. Dip one of the rice paper wrappers into a shallow bowl of warm water, then drain and lay out flat. Lay a few herb leaves across the middle, top with carrot, radish, apple and noodles, and scatter over a few slices of chili and a pinch of cress. Fold the edge nearest to you over the filling, tightly roll it away from you, tucking in the sides as you go and pressing lightly to seal, then repeat.

For the peanut dip, mix the peanut butter and 2 teaspoons of soy with the juice of 1 lime, gradually loosening with a few teaspoons of water to a good dipping consistency. Slice the summer rolls into bite-sized pieces, and serve with the peanut sauce for dunking and lime wedges for squeezing over.

Delicious with a chilled glass of dry white wine.

> Feel free to embellish these with grilled oyster mushrooms, roasted cauliflower florets or chunks of silken tofu, if you like.

ENERGY	FAT	SAT FAT	PROTEIN	CARBS	SUGARS	SALT	FIBER
319kcal	11.6g	2g	7.7g	45.2g	9.8g	0.8g	3.8g

EXCITING CRUDITÉS

TAHINI YOGURT DIP, SCALLION & PICKLED CHILI, PICKLED BEET

SERVES 6 | **20 MINUTES**

2 scallions

1 fresh green chili

white wine vinegar

1 small beet

1¼ lbs crunchy veg, such as
     fennel, celery, radishes,
     peppers, mixed-color beets,
     carrots, cucumber, daikon,
     cauliflower, green beans

1 lemon

3 tablespoons tahini

1 clove of garlic

1 cup plain yogurt

extra virgin olive oil

2 sprigs of fresh mint

Trim the scallions and chili, then chop as finely as you can and place in a small bowl with 1 tablespoon of vinegar and a good pinch of sea salt. Peel and very finely grate the beet, scrape into another bowl, then mix in 1 tablespoon of vinegar and a good pinch of salt. Leave aside to lightly pickle.

Trim and prep the crunchy veg as necessary, then slice to an agreeable bite size and place on a serving plate. Squeeze over half the lemon juice, season with salt, and toss to coat. Loosen the tahini with 1 tablespoon of boiling water and the remaining lemon juice. Peel and finely grate in the garlic, then whisk in the yogurt and drizzle with 1 tablespoon of oil. Dot the pickles onto the yogurt dip, pick over the mint leaves, and serve the veg alongside for dunking.

> The enjoyment of having crunchy raw veg is hugely amplified by a squeeze of citrus — why not try lime, blood orange or grapefruit juice next time?

ENERGY	FAT	SAT FAT	PROTEIN	CARBS	SUGARS	SALT	FIBER
126kcal	8g	1.8g	5.3g	8.6g	6.7g	1.2g	2.4g

GNARLY BLACK BEAN TACOS

COTTAGE CHEESE, SMOKY CHIPOTLE TABASCO & SCALLIONS

SERVES 4 | 10 MINUTES

1 x 15-oz can of black beans

½ teaspoon ground cumin

1 teaspoon red wine vinegar

2 small corn tortillas

2 tablespoons cottage cheese

chipotle Tabasco sauce

2 scallions

Drain the beans, then mash in a large non-stick frying pan over a medium heat with the cumin, vinegar and a pinch of sea salt and black pepper. Fry for a few minutes to get a bit of color, tossing regularly, then separate into two small piles and squash a tortilla on top of each (don't worry if they don't quite fit into the pan – they can overlap a little and still work beautifully!). Push down to flatten and stick the bean mixture to the tortilla, then squash and cook until hot through.

Carefully turn out onto a board, top with bombs of cottage cheese and a few shakes of Tabasco, to taste, then finely slice and sprinkle over the scallions, and clank up into quarters. Serve with an ice-cold beer, and relax.

> Feel free to use different types of beans, and swap out cottage cheese for Cheddar, if you prefer – it's all good!

ENERGY	FAT	SAT FAT	PROTEIN	CARBS	SUGARS	SALT	FIBER
129kcal	2.4g	0.6g	7.3g	16.6g	1.7g	0.8g	6.7g

CRISPY MOROCCAN CARROTS

ORANGE & THYME SYRUP, TAHINI & HARISSA RIPPLED YOGURT

SERVES 6 | 50 MINUTES PLUS COOLING

12 baby carrots

3 oranges

3 fresh bay leaves

3 sprigs of fresh thyme

4 sheets of phyllo pastry

olive oil

liquid honey

2 tablespoons sesame seeds

1 tablespoon tahini

2 teaspoons rose harissa

6 tablespoons plain yogurt

Preheat the oven to 400°F. Scrub the carrots, then cook in a pan of fast-boiling salted water for 10 minutes, or until just tender, then drain. Finely grate half the orange zest into the empty pan and squeeze in all the juice. Place on a medium heat, add the bay, thyme and a good pinch of sea salt, then cook until syrupy, folding the carrots back into the glaze to coat. Leave to cool.

One by one, lay out the phyllo sheets, rub with oil, then cut lengthways into 3 strips. Place a carrot at the bottom of each and roll up like a cigar, squeezing lightly to seal (don't worry about being too neat). Repeat with the remaining carrots and phyllo, placing them on a baking sheet as you go. Brush each lightly with oil, then roast for 20 minutes, or until lightly golden and crisp, drizzling with a little honey and scattering with the sesame seeds for the last 5 minutes.

Stack the carrots on a board, scattering over any sesame seeds left on the pan, then swirl the tahini and harissa through the yogurt and serve alongside.

People love this as a nibble, starter or side, and are always surprised if you use different colored heirloom carrots – pink, purple, yellow . . . whatever you like!

ENERGY	FAT	SAT FAT	PROTEIN	CARBS	SUGARS	SALT	FIBER
239kcal	11.6g	2.1g	5.1g	30g	10g	0.9g	4.3g

HINTS & TIPS

LET'S CHAT CHEESE

The world of veggie cheese is getting bigger all the time, with more and more cheesemakers embracing and experimenting with vegetarian coagulants. There's no category of cheese that is exclusively veggie – if in doubt, speak to your local cheesemonger for more information, or simply check the back of the pack before you buy. And if you're struggling to find enough choice, speak to your local supermarket to encourage them to stock some veggie alternatives.

You'll see that I've used a whole range of cheeses in this book and haven't specified using veggie. There are lots of fantastic vegetarian alternatives out there now, so if you don't want to use cheese made with animal rennet, please do swap in a suitable alternative. To source amazing British cheeses, check out Neal's Yard Dairy, which distributes all over the world.

For all the vegans out there, it's very hard to mimic the flavor and texture of cheese, but there are brands doing a great job right now, and the market is moving very quickly, so watch this space. And for the non-veggies, you've probably got more choice than ever.

A NOTE ON PARMESAN

Parmesan cheese, and anything containing it, such as store-bought pestos, will include animal rennet. Whenever I've used these ingredients, or any other non-vegetarian ingredients, I have clearly flagged them in green type on the relevant pages, just above the nutrition bar at the bottom of the page. To make these recipes fully vegetarian, look out for these notes and swap to the suggested alternatives. Also, if you want to follow a strict vegetarian diet, remember to check all packaging to ensure you're buying veggie-friendly ingredients across the board.

HERE ARE SOME WORLD-CLASS CHEESES YOU MUST LOOK OUT FOR, THAT JUST HAPPEN TO BE VEGGIE

Appleby's Cheshire

Applewood

Beenleigh Blue

Black Bomber

Blacksticks Blue

Brunswick Blue

Cardo

Cashel Blue

Cornish Yarg

Cotherstone

Riseley

Sinodun Hill

Spa Blue

Spenwood

Stinking Bishop

Ticklemore

Waterloo

Wigmore

It's really good that we have the choice of so many different milks — whether dairy or plant-based — these days. But it's important to remember that dairy milk packs a real nutrition punch, and that plant-based milk drinks aren't as clear-cut, so it's often necessary to fill the gaps.

Personally, I choose organic dairy milk, and yogurt and cheeses that come from it – it's a great-value trade-up. But here are some thoughts:

Plant-based drinks can be made from many different plants, including soya, almonds, coconuts, oats and rice – and a broad selection is increasingly available in supermarkets. Depending on how they're made, these drinks can be a good source of some nutrients. However, some almond milks are predominantly made of water (up to 80%), with some containing as little as 2% almonds. So while they can form part of a nutritious diet, drinking them as a direct replacement for cow's milk can increase the risk of missing out on some key nutrients – choose fortified, unsweetened versions to reduce the risk of deficiency.

In the UK, cow's milk provides protein, calcium, iodine and some B vitamins. Calcium is important for healthy teeth, strong bones and muscle function, and B vitamins help keep our nervous system healthy, maintain a healthy immune system and convert the food we eat into energy. Iodine is essential for making thyroid hormones, needed for metabolism, growth and the development of babies' brains during gestation and early life.

PLANT-BASED CHOICES

There are many quick and easy switches that can be made to make a dish completely plant-based, particularly when it comes to dairy.

- Fortified, unsweetened plant-based drinks are an easy switch to replace animal milk.

- Plant-based yogurts are also now widely available – soy being the most popular – and can be used instead of plain yogurt for those avoiding dairy. Again, try to choose unsweetened versions. These yogurts are a great lower-fat alternative to mayonnaise.

- Soy and dairy-free spreads can be used in place of butter; just check the ingredients lists to make sure that the product is free of "trans" or "hydrogenated" fats.

- Dairy-free cheeses are also now available.

For more information on following a vegan diet, visit jamieoliver.com/nutrition-guidance/ or seek the advice of a registered nutritionist or dietician.

It goes without saying that our fat consumption needs to be kept in check, but a healthy diet does require the right fats, so choose unsaturated sources when you can, such as olive and liquid vegetable oils, nuts, seeds and avocados (this also includes omega-3-rich oily fish).

WHAT ARE THE HEALTHIEST OILS?

The polyunsaturated fatty acids omega-3 and omega-6 are the two essential fatty acids that we need to get from our diets, because our body cannot make them. These are found in nut and seed oils (canola, walnut, flaxseed, avocado and sunflower oil) – I've mostly used olive and extra virgin olive oil on the recipe pages, but feel free to swap these into your cooking.

Different oils have different fatty-acid compositions and therefore different health benefits; however, most oils are high in a combination of monounsaturated and polyunsaturated fatty acids. When these fats replace saturated fats in our diet, they reduce and maintain healthy cholesterol levels, reducing the risk of heart disease. Some oils can boast more specific health claims, like olive oil, whose polyphenols have been proven to have protective properties. Similarly, avocado and sunflower oil are high in vitamin E, which we need for cell protection.

COCONUT OIL – WHAT'S THE DEAL?

I'm not anti coconut oil, but the fictitious health benefits associated with it, and therefore its overuse, are of concern. Coconut oil has a higher proportion of saturated fatty acids than any other plant-based oil, and is very low in essential fatty acids. My advice is to use it in moderation and only in dishes where it adds appropriate flavor.

BUTTER

Butter can be great for adding flavor to certain dishes; however, it should be used in moderation. I personally try to choose butter made from grass-fed cow's milk.

VEGAN ALTERNATIVES TO BUTTER

When it comes to margarines available on the market, just make sure to avoid any products made with trans fats – these could be labeled as "hydrogenated" or "partially hydrogenated" fats – which can be harmful to the body and are best avoided.

One of the clever little tricks I use to mimic butter is to take quality cold-pressed extra virgin olive oil and pop it into the fridge or freezer to solidify – it'll give you a naturally spreadable, healthier and delicious non-dairy alternative to butter.

Amazing vinegar can really transform a dish, and is often the unsung hero of any pantry. I enjoy flavoring my own vinegars, and would highly recommend buying large bottles of red or white wine vinegar, dividing them between smaller sterilized bottles (see page 252) and jazzing them up with all kinds of different flavors. Seal, label and pop on the shelf ready to use – brilliant in dressings and marinades, used to add magic to soups and stews, or decanted into a little spray bottle for spritzing onto anything roasted. Seriously tasty!

HERE ARE SOME OF MY FAVORITE ADDITIONS

Berries – strawberries, blueberries, blackberries, blackcurrants, cranberries

Stone fruit – cherries, plums, apricots, peaches, nectarines

Fresh herbs – mint, basil, chives, parsley, bay, rosemary, cilantro, dill, tarragon, thyme (in the summer it's quite romantic to cut flowering herbs and sink them into vinegar to capture the moment)

Honey or honeycomb

Fennel

Blends of toasted spices – cinnamon, cloves, star anise, allspice, mustard seeds, fennel seeds, peppercorns

Ginger or garlic

Fresh chilies
(Scotch bonnets if you like things fiery!)

Strips of citrus zest

Rose petals

Vanilla beans

Elderflower

For super-quick results (quicker infusion), heat up a quarter of the vinegar with your chosen seasoning, then cool and add to the rest. Brilliantly simple.

Flavor is subjective, but here are some of my favorite tips and tricks for really bolstering and getting the most out of your ingredients. These are the kinds of things I love to have ready and waiting in the fridge or cupboard, to add that extra special something and make my dishes really sing. I'm not expecting you to go out and buy all of these, but food is an adventure, so do consider picking up one new thing a week when doing your shopping.

SPICES are, by weight, some of the most nutrient-dense foods on the planet and can really make or break a meal. I use spices throughout the book for adding oomph and flavor, and when you have more flavor you need less salt, so it's a win-win. Don't be afraid to experiment with a whole array – turmeric, saffron, paprika, cinnamon, fenugreek, cumin, fennel, mustard and coriander seeds and, of course, ground chili, are some of my favorites.

FRESH HERBS are a joyful element of cooking and can really liven up your meals (not to mention their reputed nutritious qualities). Pick, chop, tear, pound, bash or muddle them together with quality extra virgin olive oil, and add to dishes for an extra layer of flavor, freshness, surprise and deliciousness. Fresh herbs really are a cook's best friend.

DRIED HERBS are a wondrous thing. The delicate, light, zingy flavors associated with fresh herbs will have disappeared, but in return you'll experience savory, robust, comforting flavors, which when added to soups, stews, sauces, breads and pulses have the ability to elevate a dish to the next level. They're super-convenient, too.

SALT is a brilliantly useful condiment that is both delightful and potentially harmful if used regularly to excess. The job of the mindful cook is to use this wonderful ingredient with respect, seasoning intelligently to bring the best out of your ingredients. Generally speaking, the easiest way to reduce your salt intake is to avoid processed fast foods and cook from scratch as often as you can. That way, you'll know exactly how much salt has been added.

FLAVORED SALT is a fun, clever way to have an array of preserved flavors just a pinch away. Simply whiz sea salt in a blender with your chosen flavors – herbs, chilies, citrus zest and juice, dried mushrooms and seaweed all brilliantly work well, to name just a few. Spread out on a baking sheet to fully dry, then bash up and keep in sealed jars for future use. By default, creating a flavored salt results in a slightly lower-salt seasoning. Happy days!

HARISSA, like any chili paste or oil, brings a wonderful background warmth to a dish. Made with ground spices and dried herbs, sometimes with preserved lemons and rose water, it adds a ray of sunshine to all kinds of dishes. Look out for it.

PICKLES, CHUTNEYS & PRESERVES provide layers of flavor, depth, surprise and crunch. Whether you're making a stir-fry, stew, tagine, curry or cheese toastie – just a little amount here and there can bring dishes to life in a fast and convenient way. To me, life without pickles is a little dull. And you can't beat a jar of veg and fruit preserved at the optimal time.

CURRY PASTES – whether buying or making your own (they freeze well in ice-cube trays), these are the most fantastic flavor bombs to have on hand. Made from a blend of herbs, spices and fragrant ingredients, there's so much flavor in just one little spoonful.

SUN-DRIED TOMATOES are available everywhere these days. Whether you choose the paste or the halved tomatoes in oil, they'll bring dynamism and sunshine to your dishes.

MISO, which is quite trendy at the moment, is a fermented soy or rice product, and there's a lot of fun to be had with it. Providing a deep umami flavor, it adds real oomph to noodle and rice dishes. Traditionally used in soups and broths, it can also be added to gravies and stews, or even tossed with veg before roasting. Enjoy experimenting.

SOY SAUCE OR TAMARI – who doesn't love a swig? These fermented products are brilliant for adding deep umami seasoning to foods. Standard and reduced-sodium versions are both brilliant – just remember to use in moderation to keep your salt intake in check.

NUTS & SEEDS can be very good for us, and a handful a day can have a real benefit because of the heart-healthy fats they contain. Brilliant crushed, crumbled, chopped or pounded into flour, they're fantastic at perking up salads, stews and curries. Use raw for added creaminess, or toast for incredible texture and nuttiness. Have fun with your nuts; don't be boring.

TAHINI is a sesame seed paste, essential in hummus. It's really good in marinades and sauces, or in breakfasts and desserts, and is perfect for drizzling and dunking, too. Delicious!

DRIED MUSHROOMS are an absolute must for big beefy, meaty flavor. I use them all the time, often instead of bouillon cubes – you get a lovely dark color and deep flavor. In Asian supermarkets you can sometimes pick up bigger bags at really great prices.

CAPERS & OLIVES are widely used around the Mediterranean. Just a small amount of these can really lift a dish, with pops of concentrated flavor. You can use them instead of salt to give you a really delicious floral savoriness. I always have some on hand, no matter what.

CRACKING CONDIMENTS, such as chili, teriyaki, Worcestershire and HP sauce, as well as things like Marmite, peanut butter and mustard, are real gems – a swig, dash or spoonful can add an accent flavor to all kinds of dishes. Use with restraint, but enjoy when you do.

Take your dishes to the next level by topping with these easy-to-create flavor gems – they're beyond simple to knock together but make all the difference.

FLAVORED BREADCRUMBS

Simply frying breadcrumbs with a little oil, herbs and garlic can add an amazing flavor, texture and dynamic to all kinds of dishes, including salads, stews and pastas, to name just a few. And with bread being one of the most wasted foods, this simple flavor-boosting preservation technique is a bit of a double whammy. Straight-up stale breadcrumbs are delicious, too.

CITRUS

Invest in a fine grater – a few scrapings of zest can really lift a dish, and also make it look beautiful. A squeeze of juice is often all that's needed to get those taste buds really dancing.

FRESH SALSAS

A good salsa, whether chunky or smooth, has the ability to add amazing color, life, tang and seasoning to so many dishes. It's a constant in my kitchen – fantastic for adding surprise and awakening the palate. My general principle is to use finely chopped herbs, ripe tomatoes and acidity – through the use of either vinegar or citrus – a little seasoning and possibly some fruit for added sweetness. Adjust the consistency to suit the dish you're embellishing.

RIPPLED YOGURTS

I quite enjoy finishing dishes with refreshing yogurt, rippled with contrasting flavor punches like spicy harissa, pestos, pastes, olives, sun-dried tomatoes, tahini, chutneys or pickles. Think of it as a yin-yang of deliciousness that matches with, and elevates, your dish.

FROZEN CHILIES

Freeze on-the-turn chilies, then finely grate over dishes for a delicate kick. Great for making marinades, and for adding a hum to sauces and stews. Ginger can be treated in the same way.

TEMPERS

A really interesting way of adding a last-minute whack of flavor to dishes, a temper, in its simplest form, is made from lightly toasted spices, herbs and fragrant ingredients heated in a little oil. Typically, it's spooned over curries, but I've also had incredible success using it with roasted veg, soups and salads. Use your imagination, and have a go.

PICKLES & CHUTNEYS

It may sound obvious, but pickles and chutneys make fantastic accompaniments. For me, things like piccalilli, mango or chili pepper chutney are the tip of the iceberg, but every culture has its own expression – whether that's super-fresh and zingy, or preserved and jarred to capture the best of the season. I'm always exploring, and love buying jars of things I don't recognize to see if I like them, and if they will work well with dishes I cook regularly. Try to create opportunities to try new flavors – it's exciting!

CHILI SAUCE

I absolutely love chilies, and I know I'm not the only one. A dash or three of chili sauce can really lift a dish – the question is, how much and what flavor? Everyone seems to be adding Sriracha to most things these days, which is super-tasty, but the key is to test out lots of different ones, until you hone in on your favorite flavors. I've even known people to collect chili sauces like souvenirs – it's a bit geeky, but I love it.

STOCK Good-quality stock is a handy thing to have in the freezer. Now, I know you can easily buy decent organic stocks these days, but for truly cracking flavor (and not a lot of effort!), try making your own. Often, a lot of the ingredients that go into making a stock are by-products or waste anyway, so it's a great way to make the most of your ingredients.

I frequently make a big batch of fresh stock, using a myriad of surplus vegetables, as well as peelings and trimmings I've saved, fresh herbs, and even the skins of roasted veg, such as celery root, carrots and parsnips. Simply pop them into a container in the freezer until you've built up enough of a collection to be able to cook up your next batch of tasty stock.

To make stock from scratch, cover the veg and any saved trimmings with water, embellishing with your chosen herbs, peppercorns, unpeeled bashed garlic cloves, and maybe a splash of wine or some additional spices. A handful of dried mushrooms thrown into the mix will also earn you big flavor points, as will things like chili, ginger, miso, tomato paste, tamari, vinegar, seaweed and soy, if you're after more of a punchy vibe, depth of flavor or accent, where applicable. Bring to a boil, then simmer gently for an hour or two until it tastes fantastic. Season to perfection with sea salt and black pepper, and sieve before using. To save for another day, leave to cool, then bag up in portions and freeze flat to minimize defrosting time. And don't forget to label and date them for future reference.

CHOOSE QUALITY As is often the case in cooking, the success of the recipes comes down to the quality of the ingredients you use. Trade up where you can, buying the best produce you can find. To this end, remember that shopping in season always allows your food to be more nutritious, more delicious and more affordable. Ingredients that noticeably make a difference on the flavor front when you choose best-quality are jarred beans and chickpeas, canned plum tomatoes, curry pastes, stock (see above to make your own), oils (see pages 272–3) and vinegars (see page 274). These are ingredients that are used in abundance in cooking, and can often be commoditized, meaning that the norm becomes the lesser-quality cheaper version. But, by rediverting some of the money saved from not buying meat, you can enjoy extraordinary gains in flavor and texture by upgrading. Money well spent, I'd say.

DAIRY & EGGS With staple dairy products, like milk, yogurt and butter, I couldn't endorse the trade-up to organic more. It is more expensive, but we're talking pennies, not pounds. Plus, every time you buy organic, you vote for a better food system. The same goes for eggs and anything containing egg, such as noodles and pasta – always choose free-range or organic.

ORGANIC IS THE NORM To this day, people are still debating organic production in comparison with what is now viewed as "normal" farming. In my mind, organic is and should be the norm – this is the way we have farmed for millennia, as opposed to relying heavily on pesticides, herbicides and other chemicals, which have sadly become a big part of the modern farming industry. Organic produce is not an option for everyone, and that is absolutely fair enough, but if you can, supporting local organic farmers is a wonderful thing to do. In doing so, I really believe that you're voting for a better food system. I don't buy 100% organic, but I do the very best I can, when I can – and that's always been the way.

EQUIPMENT I've kept the equipment I've used in this book pretty simple – a set of saucepans and non-stick ovenproof frying pans, a grill pan and a large casserole pan, chopping boards, some sturdy roasting pans, a couple of baking sheets and a decent set of knives will see you through. If you want to save time, there are a few kitchen gadgets that will make your life a lot easier – things like a vegetable peeler, a box grater and a pestle and mortar are all fantastic for creating great texture and boosting flavor, and a food processor or immersion blender and a mandolin are always a bonus, especially if you're short on time! Keep your kit in good nick, and your kitchen organized, and you'll be ready to go.

A NOTE ON FREEZING Remember to let food cool before freezing, breaking it down into portions so it cools quicker and you can get it into the freezer within 2 hours. Make sure everything is well wrapped, and labeled up for future reference. Thaw in the fridge before use. Generally, if you've frozen cooked food, don't freeze it again after you've reheated it.

NUTRITION

A NOTE FROM JAMIE'S NUTRITION TEAM

Our job is to make sure that Jamie can be super-creative, while also ensuring that all his recipes meet the guidelines we set. Every book has a different brief, and *Ultimate Veg* is a real celebration of veg-based recipes, focusing both on meals you can enjoy every day and on more indulgent foods for weekends and special occasions. 70% of the recipes in this book fit into our healthy guidelines – some are complete meals, but there'll be others that you'll need to balance out with what's lacking. For absolute clarity and so that you can make informed choices, we've presented the nutritional content for each dish (per serving) on the recipe page itself, giving you an easy access point to understand how to fit these recipes into your week.

Food is fun, joyful and creative – it gives us energy and plays a crucial role in keeping our bodies healthy. Remember, a good, balanced diet and regular exercise are the keys to a healthier lifestyle. We don't label foods as "good" or "bad," but encourage an understanding of the difference between nutritious foods for everyday consumption and those to be enjoyed occasionally.

For more info on our guidelines and how we analyze recipes, visit:

jamieoliver.com/nutrition

Rozzie Batchelar, Senior Nutritionist, RNutr (food)

A BIT ABOUT BALANCE

Balance is key when it comes to eating well. Balance your plate right and keep your portion control in check, and you can be confident that you're giving yourself a great start on the path to good health. It's important to consume a variety of foods to ensure we get the nutrients our bodies need to stay healthy. This means eating from all the food groups: vegetables; fruit; whole-grain starchy carbohydrates; protein – this of course includes lean meat and fish, but in this book we're going meat-free and heroing plant-based proteins (beans and pulses, nuts, seeds) and eggs; and naturally low-fat dairy foods and a small amount of unsaturated fats. There's a place for all kinds of food in our diet; it's about how often and how much.

WHAT'S THE BALANCE?

The UK government's Eatwell Guide shows us what a healthy balance of food looks like. Don't worry about the exact percentages, but use the figures below to think about the proportion of each food group you consume across the day.

THE FIVE FOOD GROUPS (UK)	PROPORTION*
Vegetables & fruit	39%
Starchy carbohydrates (bread, rice, potatoes, pasta)	37%
Protein (eggs, beans, other non-dairy sources – heroed in this book – as well as lean meat & fish)	12%
Dairy foods, milk & dairy alternatives	8%
Unsaturated fats (such as oils)	1%
AND DON'T FORGET TO DRINK PLENTY OF WATER, TOO	

* Please note: the remaining 3% is made up of food to be enjoyed occasionally.

VEGETABLES & FRUIT

To live a good, healthy life, veg and fruit should sit right at the heart of your diet. Different-colored vegetables and fruits come in all kinds of shapes, sizes, flavors and textures, and contain different vitamins and minerals, which each play a part in keeping our bodies healthy and optimal, so it's important to try to eat a variety each day (see pages 291–2).

STARCHY CARBOHYDRATES

Carbs provide us with a large proportion of the energy needed to make our bodies move, and to ensure our organs have the fuel they need to function. When you can, choose fiber-rich whole-grain and whole-wheat varieties. 260g is the recommended daily amount of carbohydrates for the average adult, with up to 90g coming from total sugars, which includes natural sugars found in whole fruit, milk and milk products, and no more than 30g of free sugars. Free sugars are those added to food and drink, including sugar found in honey, syrups, fruit juice and smoothies. Fiber (see page 288) is also classed as a carbohydrate, and adults should be aiming for about 30g of fiber each day.

FIBER

Fiber is important in keeping our digestive systems happy. A fiber-rich diet helps our gut microbiota flourish and helps bulk up our feces (that's right, we're talking about poo, but it's important!), meaning we can get rid of waste efficiently. Both these things equal a happy gut!

Fiber is found in plant-based foods. We can't digest fiber, but microbiota in our gut can, which helps to keep our digestive systems happy. There are two different types of fiber: insoluble fiber – which helps other food and waste pass through the gut – and soluble fiber, which helps to slow digestion and lower cholesterol.

Insoluble fiber is largely found in whole-grain foods, as well as in popcorn, potato skins, dried fruit, nuts, beans, corn, broccoli and carrots. And soluble fiber is found in oats, barley, pulses, beans, sweet potatoes, peas, apples, oranges and avocados.

Fiber helps to keep us regular, control our blood-sugar levels and maintain lower cholesterol.

PROTEIN

Think of protein as the building blocks of our bodies – it's used for everything that's important to how we grow and repair. The requirement for an average woman aged 19 to 50 is 45g per day, with 55g for men in the same age bracket.

Sources of protein of course include meat and fish, but whether you're a meat eater, vegetarian or vegan, eating more plant-based proteins can be beneficial for health, and also contribute to a more sustainable diet. Compared to protein from animal sources, plant-based protein is lower in saturated fat and salt (in the case of processed meats), and higher in fiber. Beans, pulses, nuts, seeds, tofu and any product derived from these are good sources of plant protein. For more information on following a vegetarian or vegan diet, visit jamieoliver.com/nutrition-guidance/.

Many people worry about not getting enough protein on a plant-based diet, because plant-based protein sources don't always contain all the essential amino acids and aren't absorbed as efficiently. However, if you eat a wide variety of plant-based proteins, they can still provide you with all the essential amino acids you need. Soy, hemp and quinoa are all "complete proteins," meaning they contain all the essential amino acids our bodies need.

DAIRY FOODS, MILK & DAIRY ALTERNATIVES

This little slice of a balanced plate offers an amazing array of nutrients when eaten in the right amounts. Favor milk, yogurt and small amounts of cheese in this category; the lower-fat varieties (with no added sugar) are equally brilliant and worth embracing. If opting for plant-based versions, favor the fortified, unsweetened products (see pages 270–1).

UNSATURATED FATS

While we only need small amounts, we do require healthier fats (see pages 272–3). Choose unsaturated sources where you can, such as olive and liquid vegetable oils, nuts, seeds and avocados (this also includes omega-3-rich oily fish). Generally speaking, it's recommended that the average woman has no more than 70g of fat per day, with less than 20g of that from saturated fat, and the average man no more than 90g, with less than 30g from saturates.

DRINK PLENTY OF WATER

This one is simple – to be the very best you can be, stay hydrated. Water is essential to life, and to every function of the human body! In general, females aged 14 and older need at least 8 cups per day, and males in the same age bracket need at least 10 cups per day. Lower-fat milks and unsweetened drinks like tea and coffee can also contribute to fluid intake. It's also worth mentioning that in most municipalities, tap water is completely safe and often of fantastic quality – not to mention that it can be consumed for free.

ENERGY & NUTRITION INFO

Generally speaking, the average woman needs around 2,000 calories a day, while the average man needs roughly 2,500. These figures are a guide, and what we eat needs to be considered in relation to factors like age, build, lifestyle and activity levels.

EAT THE RAINBOW

It's super-important to eat a variety of veg and fruit, as they each contain a whole spectrum of different vitamins and minerals, which all play a part in keeping our bodies healthy and happy — the list below will tell you a bit more about the benefits of eating a whole rainbow of different colors. The brilliant thing about veg and fruit is that there are still loads of hidden compounds we're yet to discover, together with the benefits they have on our bodies. Exciting times!

RED fruits, such as tomatoes, peppers and chilies, are all a source of vitamin C, which our bodies need for many different things, from maintaining healthy teeth, gums and skin to supporting immune function. Peppers and chilies are also a source of vitamin B6, which is important for metabolic and nervous-system function. Red peppers are also high in folic acid, which we need for immune function.

PINK fruits, like strawberries, raspberries and pomegranates, aren't too dissimilar to red fruits in that they provide a source of vitamin C and are also often a source of vitamin B6 — pomegranates, for example. Some, like strawberries, are also a source of folic acid, which we need to make red blood cells and to prevent tiredness and fatigue.

ORANGE veg and fruit — think carrots, squash, sweet potatoes, oranges — provide sources of vitamin E, vitamin C and vitamin A. Beta carotene, a form of vitamin A, is what gives them their orange color, and this is important for maintaining normal vision. Our bodies need vitamin E for cell protection.

YELLOW veg and fruit, such as yellow peppers, yellow zucchini and corn, contain folic acid, which our bodies need for many different things, like metabolic and immune function. Yellow peppers, like their red versions, are also high in vitamin C, while corn also provides a source of thiamin, which our hearts need in order to function. The popular banana is a source of potassium and vitamin B6, while lemon juice provides vitamin C.

GREEN veg provide us with a wide variety of nutrients. Folic acid is found in a large number of green veg and is needed for many different functions, including red blood cell formation and helping to prevent tiredness and fatigue, as well as for immune and metabolic function.

Vitamin K is found in very high amounts in kale in particular, but also in broccoli, green beans and other green veg. Vitamin K is important for maintaining healthy bones.

Potassium, found in lots of green veg, like zucchini and fennel, is important for maintaining our blood pressure and for muscle and nervous-system function.

DARK GREEN leafy veg in particular, like spinach, can also be a source of calcium and iron.

PURPLE veg and fruit – think eggplants, red grapes, red cabbage – contain potassium, which we need for maintaining healthy blood pressure and muscle function. Some can also be a source of vitamin C, in the case of red cabbage and cherries, and blueberries are high in manganese, which we need for maintaining bone health.

BRILLIANT BEANS & PULSES

Beans and pulses come in all different colors, shapes and sizes, and with that offer an array of different nutrients. As well as contributing to daily veg, they also provide us with a source of fiber and are high in protein, so are a great meat alternative to switch in. The type of fiber found in beans and pulses is "soluble fiber," which contributes to lowering and maintaining healthy cholesterol, helping to protect us against heart disease. On top of this, they are also a source of important micronutrients – for example, lentils and kidney beans are a great source of iron. The type of iron found in plant-based foods is harder for our bodies to absorb compared to that found in animal products, so it's best to consume them with foods high in vitamin C to increase absorption.

HOW MUCH SHOULD WE EAT?

In the UK, the guidance is to try to aim for at least 5 portions of veg or fruit each day, and at the moment only 31% of adults and 8% of 11- to 18-year-olds are meeting this target. Guidance differs from country to country – personally, I'm more in agreement with the Australian guidelines, which advise eating 5 portions of veg and 2 portions of fruit each day. The benefits of eating more veg and fruit are clear to see, so wherever in the world you live, the big message is: the more – and the more variety – the merrier!

WHAT COUNTS AS A PORTION?

A portion is considered to be 3 oz of fresh, frozen or canned veg or fruit (or a large handful), 1 oz of dried fruit (only 1 portion each day), or ⅔ cup of unsweetened veg or fruit juice (only 1 portion each day). In general, it's better to eat your veg and fruit than to drink them. Although ⅔ cup of veg and fruit juice/purée can contribute to your 5-a-day, once puréed the naturally occurring sugars become free sugars – the type of sugar more detrimental to our health if we consume too much. If you do have a juice or make a smoothie, try to choose lower-sugar options – for example, a vegetable juice rather than a fruit juice. 3 oz of beans or pulses (3 big tablespoons) counts, too (but only 1 portion each day), and also gives us protein.

IF YOU GROW IT, YOU'LL EAT IT

In my experience, if you grow something, you're far more likely to eat it – this applies to kids and adults alike! I believe that the closer you are to nature and where your food comes from, the happier and healthier you'll be – a little bit of growing can be good for the soul.

If you've never tried growing your own, I recommend giving it a go. It's inspiring, super-fun, keeps you fit and can save you money. Plus, if you've got kids, it will get them engaged in food in the most dynamic way. You don't need a garden or a field to get involved – a window box, flat roof, allotment, balcony, pot, grow-bag or bucket all work fine.

When you pick stuff straight from the ground, it's at its freshest and most nutritious. I get a geeky buzz about turning something that's been in the ground just minutes before into a meal. If you've got a farmers' market nearby and you know stuff's been picked that morning, take advantage of it. As soon as veg are picked, their nutrient levels start to deplete, so eating them as fresh as possible is going to give you more goodness per mouthful.

THANK YOU!

I started writing this book eight years ago, and from growing and cooking veggies at home with my little ones (who are not so little now), right up to now where I've traveled to extraordinary veg-loving parts of the world, it's been a truly fantastic, eye-opening experience – check out the pics over the page. It's really made me focus on the cooking techniques required to make veg some of the most delicious foods on the planet. So, from the bottom of my heart, thanks to everyone who's put up with me on this brilliant vegtastic journey.

To my food team, headed up by the wonderful Ginny Rolfe (don't forget the 5-second rule!) – 20 years together and still going strong! You are all such talented, caring, committed cooks and I'm blessed to work with you and call you my dear friends. To my in-house team: Christina Mackenzie, Maddie Rix, Jodene Jordan, Elspeth Allison, Sophie Mackinnon, Rachel Young, Hugo Harrison and Sharon Sharpe (who inspired the Pumpkin rice recipe on page 116). To Athina Andrelos, Bianca Koffman and the elegant Helen Martin – thanks for keeping us all in check. And to my freelance team: Abi Fawcett (Where's my crabs? Don't forget the IOU!), Isla Murray and India Whiley-Morton.

And big love to my Scottish brother Pete Begg (#haufnhauf) and the lovely Bobby Sebire.

Huge thanks to my brilliant nutrition gals, Rozzie Batchelar, Jenny Rosborough and Maria Parisi, for the laborious love, care and attention spent on creating absolute clarity on the nutrition front, on every page of this book. You have surpassed yourselves, again.

To my amazing editorial team, led by the lovely Beth Stroud, and to Chloe Lay and the rest of the words gang – thanks for all your hard work and dedication, as always.

And to the one and only legend and photographic genius David Loftus – it's been a pleasure and a joy to make this book together. The simplicity and honesty of the work speaks for itself. Shout-out to Richard Clatworthy on lighting and digital. To Paul Stuart, who shot the front cover and portraits – thanks for being a top man and loads of fun – great work! And a shout-out to Lima O'Donnell and Julie Akeroyd, too.

On design, big thanks to James Verity at creative agency Superfantastic – it continues to be a joy to work with you, your proficiency and amazing talent. You're getting quite annoying now – you haven't dropped the ball once!

On to my beloved publishing family at Penguin Random House. John Hamilton, it's with utter sadness that you'll never see this, but your friendship and commitment during the creation of this book was profoundly important, right up to the very last shoot day, which was joyful, productive and brilliant. We all laughed so hard it hurt. Thank you for everything. You'll be sorely missed by all. In hard times, you realize who your friends are. Many of the names below have been with me for years and I'm super grateful for the love, care and attention you always give me and my books. So much love to Tom Weldon, Louise Moore, Elizabeth Smith, Clare Parker, Annabel Wilson, Jenny Platt, Juliette Butler, Katherine Tibbals, Nick Lowndes, Christina Ellicott, Rachel Myers, Katie Corcoran, Louise Blakemore, Chantal Noel, Anjali Nathani, Catherine Wood, Lucy Beresford-Knox, Lee-Anne Williams, Antony De Rienzo, Chris Wyatt, Tracy Orchard, Stuart Anderson, Joanna Whitehead and Anna Curvis. Also to our regular freelancers, the very gorgeous Annie Lee, Sarah Day, Emma Horton and Caroline Wilding.

To my terrific marketing and PR teams: Jeremy Scott, Laura Ball, Katie McNeilage, Michelle Dam, Saskia Wirth and Ellen Diamond. And to Subi Gnanaseharam and her cracking team on social. Big love to my CEO Paul Hunt, Deputy Louise Holland, Chief Content Officer Zoe Collins, my PA, the extraordinarily brilliant Ali Solway, and to John Dewar for years of patience. Thanks to all my other teams back at HQ: technical, art, digital video, personal, legal, operations, IT, finance, P&D and facilities. You're all the best.

Thanks to my TV team – I'm blessed to work with some truly talented people. The thunder crackers that are Samantha Beddoes and Katie Millard, and their troop of incredible editorial talent: Dave Minchin, Shayma Alsayed, Maegan Tillock, Sunny Hussain. Our glorious director Niall Downing and the fantastic crew: Olly Wiggins, Luke Cardiff, Jon Kassel, Mike Sarah, Freddie Claire, Calum Thomson, Rob Thomas, Jim McLean, Ben Banayo, Alice Sephton, Julia Bell and Serena Buselli. To Sean Moxhay (you deserve a medal for holding all these creatives together), and to Anna Selby, Emily Wood and Lucy Taylor on production. And thanks also to the gang at Channel 4 and the wonderful team at FremantleMedia International.

And last but not least, big love and thanks to my nearest and dearest for putting up with me. To my darling wife, Jools, who has fully enjoyed the development of the recipes in the creation of this book. And to Poppy, Daisy, Petal, Buddy and River, who always get a plate of veggies or salad before they get anything else and now have a pretty good relationship with food (you could definitely help more with the washing-up, though!). To my incredible mum and dad, who have consistently been an amazing inspiration to me – thank you for everything! To my sweet sister Anna-Marie, and mother-in-law, Mrs. Norton, and Leon – you're the best. And to Gennaro Contaldo – why you cooking so good?

Over and out, guys . . . until next time. Jamie Trevor Oliver, MBE

INDEX

For a quick reference list of all the vegan, dairy-free and gluten-free recipes in this book, please visit: **jamieoliver.com/veg/reference**

BOOKS BY JAMIE OLIVER

Food photography DAVID LOFTUS

Cover and portrait photography PAUL STUART

Design JAMES VERITY at SUPERFANTASTIC

Recipe photography copyright © 2019 by Jamie Oliver Enterprises Limited

Cover and portrait photography copyright © 2019 Paul Stuart

Illustrations copyright © 2019 by Jon Gray (page 3)

© 2007 P22 Underground Pro Demi, all rights reserved P22 type foundry, Inc.

Food photography by David Loftus

Travel photography by Freddie Claire (page 296–297)

Color reproduction by Altaimage Ltd.

Designed by Superfantastic

jamieoliver.com
www.flatironbooks.com

The Library of Congress Cataloging-in-Publication Data is available upon request.

ISBN 978-1-250-26288-2 (paper over board)
ISBN 978-1-250-26722-1 (ebook)

Our books may be purchased in bulk for promotional, educational, or business use. Please contact your local bookseller or the Macmillan Corporate and Premium Sales Department at 1-800-221-7945, extension 5442, or by email at MacmillanSpecialMarkets@macmillan.com.

Originally published in the United Kingdom in 2019 by Michael Joseph, an imprint of Penguin Books Ltd.

Previously published in Canada by HarperCollins Publishers Ltd.

First U.S. Edition: January 2020

10 9 8 7 6 5 4 3 2 1

HUNGRY FOR MORE?

For handy nutrition advice, as well as videos, features, hints, tricks and tips on all sorts of different subjects, loads of brilliant recipes, plus much more, check out

JAMIEOLIVER.COM   #JAMIESVEG